D1572481

DANCING IN THE EYE OF TRANSFORMATION

TEN KEYS TO CREATIVE CONSCIOUSNESS

Personal and Planetary Transformation
Through Mind-Body-Spirit Integration

SYLVIA BRALLIER

ILLUSTRATED BY
KIVA SINGH AND SYLVIA BRALLIER

Triple Muse Publications
www.triplemuse.com
Las Vegas, NV

Dancing in the Eye of Transformation
10 Keys to Creative Consciousness
by Sylvia Brallier

Copyright © 2006 Sylvia Brallier
1st Printing, 2006
ISBN, print ed.   0-97798-430-3

Triple Muse

Publications

Triple Muse Publishing
Las Vegas, NV
www.triplemuse.com
info@triplemuse.com
(866)357-1843

Illustrations and Fine Art by Kiva Singh,   www.kivasingh.com
Cover Graphic by Mikio Kennedy,   www.merlinswheel.com

Dedication

Dedicated to my remarkable parents whose unconditional love, support and wisdom helped me to be the best parts of who I am today.

Thanks

Special thanks to Kiva Singh, Melissa Wilreker, Tobias Beckwith, Adele Rae, Dr. Anne Key, Todd Karr, Mikio Kennedy, Abraham Street, Julie Woods, Katlyn Breene, Abigail Spinner McBride, Dragon, and Nemea Arborvitae for their invaluable help in the creation of this book.

Table of Contents

Introduction

My life is a story of weaving.

All of my life, I have been a spiritual seeker fascinated by the various mystical traditions of the world. I have always marveled at the amazing diversity that springs from different cultures and beliefs. There is so much beauty in the many ways to be a human. There have been wise ones and great healers in every culture. I have reveled in that diversity and have found ways to weave those wisdoms into my life. These teachings have enriched me beyond measure.

As a spiritual healer, I work with many different people with many different cultural and spiritual backgrounds. I feel it is important for me to work with each person in a way that honors that person's unique perspective and background instead of trying to make them fit into mine. The study and practice of these different paradigms helped me to serve each person in the way that would work best for them instead of attempting to fit a square peg in a round hole. While I could not possibly practice all the disciplines of every tradition I have been a part of on a regular basis, I have been able to weave the parts that seem to flow together well to make a cohesive whole that is my unique paradigm, not unlike a beautiful tapestry.

Some people have asked me what tradition I am a part of. I suppose the most truthful answer would be that I am philosophically closest to a Buddhist. My daily practices are Hindu Tantric. My community is predominantly eclectic pagans, and my healing and teaching work incorporates all of these facets along with shamanic practices, bio-energetic, vibrational and hypno-therapeutic modalities.

As I formed my spiritual world view, I have come to the conclusion that reality is totally subjective. While I have done my best to view reality from an open mind, some concepts just didn't fit into the personal paradigm I was creating. As a result, they got left out of the sacred stew I was cooking up. The idea that Divinity was only male didn't seem right, so that got dropped. I couldn't fathom that there was only "one way" to enlightenment and salvation. I have met and heard of so many people with different beliefs who were enlightened, so that didn't fit. I have had way too much personal evidence of the unseen realms to believe that reality is only what can be proven though linear means. Basically, what got dropped from my paradigm were beliefs that were based on exclusivity, versus inclusivity. As far as I'm concerned, it's fine for people to believe whatever they like, as long as it doesn't hurt anyone else and allows every person the right to believe and practice spirituality in her or his own unique way.

The weaving of various traditional thoughts, beliefs and practices can be a controversial approach. Some say it prevents real deepening with any one path. Some consider it "spiritual shopping," and figure it's a consumerist approach to spirituality. Some people see it as an evolution of consciousness, and others see it as a devolution. Regardless of what anyone else thinks, I feel content and aligned with my woven path. I've definitely got a lot of company. People who seek integrative approaches to healing and spirituality comprise one of the fastest growing body of seekers in the world today. Holistic approaches to personal development are the leading edge of transformative processes.

Integrative spirituality is a relational approach that recognizes that we are all a part of much larger systems than we can currently apprehend. Those who seek spiritual integration aspire to reconcile different and even sometimes opposing, beliefs and to meld practices of various schools of thought in order to affirm an underlying unity, creating a meta-paradigm of inclusivity. Integrative spirituality honors the richness of diversity within the vastness of the oneness.

The implications of this way of thinking are vast. Our very survival is likely to be dependent on our ability to perceive and honor our interconnectedness with each other and the Earth. Perhaps the awareness that we are all interconnected and interdependent can heal the fragmentation that pits nation against nation, religion against religion and humanity against nature.

> Personal transformation can and does have global effects. As we go, so goes the world, for the world is us. The revolution that will save the world is ultimately a personal one. [1]
> - Marianne Williamson

The ability to approach all of life from a holistic perspective can transform every level of our experience. For example, I believe that healing the psyche and spiritual growth are synergistically linked. All levels of the self are evolving as an interlinked system of development. It is not enough to be knowledgeable about spiritual practices and the workings of arcane rites. It is equally valuable to know the complex workings of the psyche. This powerful self-awareness can transform the relationship between the mind and the emotions, making it possible to be a person who radiates the beauty and power of a healed psyche. Every time I meditate, I experience a healing. More truth, power, energy and wholeness are created and maintained within the vehicle called 'me.' Meditation is an act of healing, whether I intend it that way or not. Similarly, when I am present for a powerful piece of healing work, I am constantly awed by the immense spiritual power present. Healing and spirituality are woven together inextricably as the warp and the woof on the loom of change.

The metaphysical principles covered in the book are very loosely based on the principles of numerology.[2] Having a system of correspondences can be helpful in order to organize diverse concepts in such a way that they can be held and comprehended simultaneously.

Each chapter can stand alone, and yet together, they represent a dynamic interplay that can assist in the integration of many layers of the psyche and synergize one's approach to enlightenment. You may have a strong affinity for some aspects and not for others. Please take what works for you and leave the rest. This book is not meant to be the creation of a new meta-religion. It is merely a guide to ways in which one might conceptualize the nesting of systems in order to find ways to view metaphysical reality from a holistic perspective.

> Believe nothing, no matter where you read it, or
> who said it, no matter if I have said it, unless it agrees
> with your own reason and your own common sense.[3]
> -Gautama Buddha

Knowledge is a funny thing. No matter how much you have learned, it's not totally real until it has been integrated into the body energetic. In order to do that, I highly recommend doing the meditations in the book.

> However many holy words you read, however
> many you speak, what good will they do you if you
> do not act upon them?
> - Buddha, from the Dhammapada

You might find the companion spoken word CD of the meditations in *Dancing in the Eye of Transformation* helpful. If you'd like to purchase it, the order form is on the back page of this book. MP3 versions are also available on our web site at: www.triplemuse.com.

Some Suggestions for Reading this Book

Some people pick up a book, and read it cover to cover. Some people buy books, but don't read them. Some start a book, and then never finish it. If you are a cover to cover person, you know what to do.

For those of you who would like to read this book, but have a hard time sticking with any book, I have a solution for you. This book lends itself to being picked up to and read at any point. Each chapter will stand alone. The same goes for most of the sub-chapters. Look and see what piques your interest and read that section. May your inspiration guide you to the information that will most serve you.

It is my prayer and desire that this book offers you keys to unlock your ability to experience and creatively express the Divine within you. Feel the truth within you. Your heart contains all the answers you'll ever need.

*The Orobouros is a symbol of infinity,perfection,
and the union of the earthly and the celestial.*

All is One and One is All

The Infinite Universe and the Ultimate Unity

Have you ever tried to imagine the universe going on forever? It's pretty hard to fathom, isn't it? We are accustomed to thinking in terms of limitation. The concept of an infinite universe is outside the scope of our perception because our perception is largely dictated by the "rules" of third-dimensional reality. Our perception defines our view of reality. What if we could think in an unlimited way? Could we expand our minds to encompass more of the universe? Would it change our reality for the better?

It seems likely that it would.

One represents the sum and the essence of all possibilities. Within it is the primordial unity of all things. No matter how many ways we try to categorize and divide the different things in the universe, there is still only one essential wholeness, which is the totality of all that is. No matter how many ways you cut up a pie, it is still a pie. The universe is an incredibly large thing, beyond perception. Perhaps if we could fathom the universe, we could fathom the Divine, God, Goddess, Spirit, vital energy...

whatever you like to call that ineffable force. From now on I'll mainly call that force "the Divine." That seems to sum it up in a way that might require the least amount of translation to the paradigm of your choice.[1]

In the Center Ring: Truth versus Dogma

Throughout the centuries, many seekers and philosophers have tried to figure out *the* truth about the Divine and the nature of reality. Some feel they have found it. Strangely enough, each one's path has been different than the others'. The good news is, there is no one right path to enlightenment. Unfortunately, the bad news is, there is no one right path to enlightenment.

The search for the one true truth has created many dogmatic systems that are at odds with each other about what the truth really is. So many people are committed to perceiving reality from a dualistic perspective based on right versus wrong. Dogma is the central tenet at the root of much of the strife in the world. Dogma has a tendency to stifle the ability to see Divinity in all its forms. These exclusionary concepts of reality do not allow for the infinite expressions of the Divine in all its varied possibilities.

It is extremely difficult for human beings to perceive reality objectively. Our perception of truth is colored by subjective reality. We are by nature beings that perceive the world around us through the lens of our individual experience and what we have been taught. Due to this condition, it is almost impossible to perceive ultimate truth for all beings without our filter getting in the way of complete perception. The best we can do is to be true to what seems right to us, and allow others to do the same.

Imagine people from around the world sitting in a circle looking at a rock that is in the center of the group. One person says "The rock is solid gray and triangular." Another person says, "The rock is light gray, and has a white streak through it." Yet another person says," The rock is long and has white spots on it."

All these people are describing the same rock, and all of these people are right. We all sit in different perspectives in relation to the rock of truth. To see outside our dogmatic systems, we need to get up and walk around the rock in order to broaden our perception of reality. This is the key to developing a multidimensional perspective.

"... Move beyond any attachment to names. Every war and every conflict between human beings has happened because of some disagreement about names. It's such an unnecessary foolishness, because just beyond the arguing there's a long table of companionship, set and waiting for us to sit down. What is praised is one, so the praise is one too many jugs being poured into a huge basin. All religions, all this singing, one song. The differences are just illusion and vanity. Sunlight looks slightly different on this wall than it does on that wall and a lot different on this other one, but it is still one light. We have borrowed these clothes, these time-and-space personalities, from a light, and when we praise, we pour them back in.

— Mevlana Jelaluddin Rumi

Of Course I'm Right! My Ego Says So, So It Must Be True!

The ego is the part of us that is particularly fascinated and completely engaged with being "right." The ego gets even craftier as we advance along the spiritual path. Some say that spiritual ego is the most difficult type of ego to conquer. This is why "beginner's mind" is so very important. It is an empty vessel in which new knowledge may be poured. Once we think we have it all figured out, we tend to get rigid in our way of perceiving things. Since our reality is limited by our perception, it is probably a good idea to keep an open mind so as not to miss out on the potential benefits of expanded thinking.

A person might not agree with what you believe, but not agreeing with you does not necessarily make them or you "wrong" or "right." What one person believes to be true may be absolutely true for that person, but it is not for anyone else to say what the right path is for someone else. Truth is relative to the perceiver. The more we can frame things in terms of "This works for me," or "This is what so-and-so believes," instead of "This is the right way, and this is the wrong way," the more we move away from polarizing and dualism, which was our original separation from divinity in the first place.

Change is the only Constant.
Go with the Flow and Get Flexible

We live in times of rapid change. In truth, change is the only constant. Just look at how many vast changes have happened in the world in the last 100 years! Both the inner and outer worlds of our experience are in a time of extreme acceleration of transformation. We are in the crux of two eras; one that is dying, and one that is bursting forth into existence. More than ever, it is important to learn the skill of flexibility. This flexibility can apply to our spiritual perception of reality as well as our physical reality. If we can be conceptually flexible, it can enable us to see and make connection with more aspects of the Divine. I believe it is more productive to see how our varied beliefs can work together instead of being divisive.

This time of change brings the gift of synthesis and an opportunity for harmony. With the advent and advancement of communications technology, the world is growing smaller every day. It is now possible to learn about the lives, customs, and beliefs of people around the world on a level never before realized on the planet.

In order to live in harmony, it would be helpful for us to focus more on what we have in common than on the matters that divide us. If we can foster global relationships built on mutual respect, trust, and understanding regardless of differences in culture, status, gender, philosophy, or religion, I have faith that we can heal our planet and ourselves.

I hope you will think of yourself as a human being rather than just as an American, or a Westerner, or a member of a particular group. These things are secondary. If you and I interact as human beings, we can reach this basic level. If I say "I am a monk; I am a Buddhist," these are, in comparison to my nature as a human being, temporary. To be human is basic. Once you are born as a human being that cannot change until your death. Other characteristics, (like) whether you are educated or uneducated, rich or poor- are secondary." [3]

— His Holiness the Dalai Lama

Converging Paradigms

The word *religion* literally means 're-linking.' Primarily, it refers to re-linking ourselves to the Divine. I like to think of religion or spirituality as a means to harmonize or link with all things. It can mean harmonizing all the parts of the self, all people with each other and the Earth and ultimately, with the Universe.

I am a fan of *syncretistic* philosophy. I don't believe that there is a one path or one way of doing things, but I seek the points of similarity that draw us together and connect us as one. Any path is just a system to try to understand or order reality. They are all just collections of symbols and concepts configured in order to attempt to grasp the mystery of the Divine order with the mind. Ultimately, this is truly impossible because the mystery is so much larger than the mind alone can conceive of.

Our mind is such a small part of who we are. But I say, as long as we have a mind, we might as well have some fun with it! I think it is important to not get too serious about trying to be right. You can only find what is right for you; you can't really find what is right in the empirical sense because there is no one right way. In my search for "rightness" I seek that which brings about harmony, balance and understanding based on compassion. This is the highest alignment with the truth I can come up with so far in my own path as a seeker.

This book is a metaphysical outline of the conclusions I've come to about how reality works. I hope you will take what works for you, and disregard the rest. It is my hope that it will help you to become clearer about your own perception of reality, and assist you to experience harmony within yourself, and the world around you.

I am deeply intrigued by spiritual systems that honor the divinity of the earthly realm as well as the celestial realm. I view everything as ultimately a part of the Divine, so seeing both the earthy and the celestial as holy is a natural conclusion for me. Many traditional tribal cultures of the world have a version of this world view as a part of their philosophy.

We can learn a great deal from these other cultures and explore the concepts, archetypes, and ceremonies that they have used for centuries. However, we can never truly have the same world view or spiritual perspective of Native Americans, Eastern Indians, Africans, Aborigines, and Tibetans etc. unless we are born to those cultures. Their symbol systems are unique to their culture so a perspective from outside of the culture will invariably be different.

By observing the many symbols, systems, and the varied traditions of the world in a respectful way, we can learn invaluable lessons not otherwise available within our own paradigm. This way, we can decide on our own concept of reality from a more unlimited perspective. From the building blocks of traditional wisdom combined with our own personal experience, we can more clearly define our own unique paradigm that embraces a larger world view of the truth. [4]

To determine your symbology is to determine your relationship to things. When you figure out what a symbol means to you, you find your relationship to it. Your attention and intention on any symbol and its meaning empowers its ability to affect your life, and also gives the essence of that symbol a greater ability to affect the collective consciousness.

A Metaphysical Unified Field Theory

Physicists have been working to develop a Unified Field Theory for many years. Einstein spent 40 years of his life trying to come up with a simple equation that would uniformly apply to the four known forces in nature (the electrostatic, strong nuclear, weak nuclear, and gravitational forces) in order to explain the nature and behavior of all matter and energy. The Unified Field Theory is based in the belief that all physical phenomena should ultimately be explainable by some common underlying natural law. If a Unified Field Theory could be proven and decoded, it could potentially unlock the secrets of nature and open incredible doors of possibility. According to Michio Kaku, a theoretical physicist from the City University of New York, those in pursuit of a Unified Field Theory seek "an equation an inch long that would allow us to read the mind of God."[5] I believe that they will one day find a way to validate the Unified Field Theory because of my own particular metaphysical belief that the Divine is both everything and one thing simultaneously. I have heard it said that Magic is just science that has not yet been explained. I do not see science and physics as separate from spiritual philosophy. The sciences are humanity's attempt to understand the mind and means of God.

Morphic Field Theory

Another field theory which I have a special affinity for is Rupert Sheldrake's morphic field resonance theory. He believes that there are resonance fields that interconnect and govern the behavior and evolution of species. His theories were developed based on the study of plant biology, migratory bird 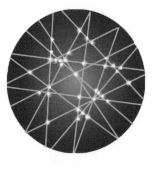 flight patterns, and studies on human and animal telepathy.

His research asks some interesting questions to which morphic resonance and formative causation appear to be good answers. When birds flock together, how do they know to turn all at once? Is a hive a group of individuated ants or bees, or is there a collective consciousness at work? Why do dogs always know when their owners are coming home? How do you know when someone is looking at you? How does telepathy work? And one of my own favorite questions, "Why do we yawn at the same time?" One of the ways these questions could be explained is by the existence of a psychic resonance or field of awareness within a species.

We are all connected whether we know it or not. All our thoughts, feelings and actions affect the whole. It has been theorized that if enough people hold a particular belief or ideal, it can create exponential change through sympathetic thought resonance.

Nested Morphic Fields

Sheldrake has theorized about morphic fields in our bodies and among species, but isn't our whole planet's ecosystem an organism? If there are morphic resonances within our bodies and within each species, it would stand to reason that there would also be a field of resonance that maintains interconnectivity between all of the species. Extrapolating further, it would also stand to reason that there would be a field of resonance that encompasses the entire organism of the planet, the galaxies, and ultimately, the universe. Things that are true on a microcosmic level are often also true on a macrocosmic level. If field theories are correct, we are inextricably woven with all that is. [6]

Consensual Reality and Natural Law

Reality is a joint construct in which we all participate. There are many ways that we each see reality very differently from one another. There are also some ways in which we have a consensual reality about how things seem to work. This might be called Natural Law. Natural laws are the things that appear to be constants, though perhaps the laws can change if our collective perception of how reality is constructed changes.

In fourth-dimensional reality, it is believed that simultaneous time exists, as opposed to the linear time construct of the third dimension. You could liken it to the many channels available on a television set. Just a small change in frequency, and *Whammo!* A whole different way of seeing things is present. All the channels exist simultaneously. Perhaps it would be like taking a walk around that rock I was talking about earlier. In simultaneous time, we could perceive all the different sides of the rock simultaneously, and thus see it from a holographic perspective. This multidimensional perspective would deeply alter our way of seeing things, and vastly expand our limited perceptions.

I like to think that, as a species, we are at a point of our evolution where we are more aware of fourth-dimensional reality as it directly affects our third-dimensional reality. From a perspective of the fourth-dimensional reality, it is likely that we would be more aware of the relationship between energy, thought and matter, due to an ability to perceive reality from a more holographic perspective.

Apparent Natural Laws

Let's look at some of the metaphysical laws that seem to directly effect our reality:

• There are those that believe in fate and destiny and those that believe we create our reality. I am definitely in the second camp. In the Free Will Zone, we create our reality through choice. Thought becomes reality. What we believe about life is what comes to pass. Some might ask: "then why are all these weird things happening in my life that I don't actually want or never thought about consciously?" It is not just the conscious mind that directs the creation of reality, but also the subconscious mind. If we do not exercise the power to consciously direct the creation of reality, whatever subconscious beliefs we hold about the nature of reality will manifest. Positive thought creates positive reality. If thought is truly the basis by which we create our lives, then the quality of those thoughts gains a much greater significance. Our self-limitations are not created by life; they are created by our negative belief systems.

• Our lives are a mirror for our consciousness. It is the ultimate feedback system. How we perceive reality is exactly what we get from life. Let's say that you are a person who believes that the world is a dangerous place and people are out to get you. You will invariably run into a situation in which someone is attempting to undermine you or hurt you in some way, thereby fulfilling your reflections on life. It does not necessarily mean that person's belief is the ultimate truth. It means that reality is completely subjective. To this person their belief appears to be is the absolute truth. For every theory you have, the universe can help you to fulfill it. It is your own filter on reality that brings things to pass.

• The law of Karma can be likened to the law of cause and effect. If you stick your finger in a flame, you will get burned. For every action, there will be some type of effect. Both thought *and* action can create tangible effects. Thought is always the initiator before we take an action, whether the thought is a conscious or an unconscious one.

If we focus on awakening our awareness and bring the light of consciousness to our unconscious, we have a greater ability to create positive and conscious manifestation within our lives. Sometimes people talk about karma in a very fatalistic way, "It's my karma, it can't be helped." Another way of viewing karma is as a latent tendency of the mind. When we apply consciousness to those latent tendencies, we can lessen or transmute those tendencies to ones that are more pleasing.

• The setting of intention is an important part of achieving a desired manifestation. A clear intent creates a clear pattern for the universe to build upon.

An architect who creates a lovely blueprint is more likely to get the building of his dreams than someone who just tells the builder "Build me a house." The clearer we are about what we actually want, the more likely we are to get it. When we are vague with the universe, the universe mirrors back a vague response. Apply care in what you ask for, as you are likely to get it.

• From a multidimensional perspective, there is no time, though here in third-dimensional reality, our perception is heavily influenced by the notions of time and space. Positive manifestation is most likely to occur if we imagine what we want to see happen as occurring in present time. When we focus on the past or focus on the future, our thought and our energy are not available in the present time. Present time is where all the magic is.

• The physical realm is the realm of manifestation in the third dimension. In the physical realm, hard work equals accomplishment. The *causal realm* is the nexus point between the wish, thought or dream, and manifestation in the physical realm. It is the dimension in which pure energy begins its descent into manifested form. The rules in the causal realm are different than the physical realm. When we relax, exercise positive thought and positive expectation regarding manifestation, we are more likely to achieve accomplishment.

• We are God, the Divine being made manifest. Anything about us that we perceive as *not* God is just a part of us that has forgotten our true nature. We are in the process of remembering our own divinity; not fixing something that is broken. This is a positive perspective that can facilitate health, well-being, enlightenment, and the manifestation of the fullest possibility of our highest potential. There is nothing that exists that is not a part of this Divine being. Our perceived fall from grace occurred as soon as we believed ourselves as somehow separate from the Infinite. We already live in Eden but our eyes are blind to see it. Everything that we need, all possibilities are available to us if we could but open our eyes and see our true nature.

• We are woven together in an intricate tapestry of enormous complexity and beauty. Every situation is an opportunity for growth and understanding. Every moment of your life is a meditation; there is no separation from the Divine. All things come from the Source. Our spiritual path is reflected in our every feeling, thought and action. Physical, emotional, psychological, intellectual and spiritual growth are all aspects of the Divine. There is no way to depart from the Oneness, no matter what we have done, said, thought, or felt. When we act out of fear and anger, we may be swimming against the Harmonic Flow, yet we have never left the river. It will only take us longer to get where we are trying to go. The Divine has eternal patience in an infinite Universe.

The Yin and Yang of it All

Night/day, earth/sky, black/white, female/male. These are but a few of the polarities that represent duality.

Many people have a way of seeing reality in a polarized manner, which essentially breaks the world in two. We can get in the habit of making judgments of right versus wrong and good versus bad as a way of defining reality instead of perceiving divergences as different yet equal. Cultivating the ability to accept *paradox* opens the way for mutual acceptance of differences, which create opportunities for peaceful coexistence between people.

The T'ai Chi Tu, or yin yang symbol from the Taoist tradition, is a symbol for the balance of the active and receptive principles. The Taoist words that describe these principles are *yin* for the receptive principle and *yang* for the active principle. When these two forces are in balance, the dynamic flow of creation is harmonized. The balancing of active and receptive energies is central to the principles of Divine alchemy as practiced by the mystical traditions of the world.

To understand the dynamic of duality a little better, let's examine some of the qualities and metaphors that describe these two principles.

Yin	**Yang**
Intuition	Intellect
Magnetic	Radiating
Receptive	Active
The void	The creation
Energy-filled emptiness	Awakened awareness
Being	Doing
Cyclical	Linear
Female	Male
Simultaneous	Sequential
To receive	To give
Right-brain thought	Left-brain thought
Diffuse awareness	Focused consciousness

We are All Both Male and Female

All people, whether male or female, have both receptive and active qualities. Each person is a synthesis of active and receptive behaviors, energies, and attributes. We incarnate in either a male or female body to integrate the lessons available to us by being a man or a woman. Most people, having incarnated into human form many times, have been both male and female in the course of their many lifetimes. By both tapping into our soul knowledge of our dual nature, and by applying our awareness to the active and receptive principles within us, we can more easily achieve a state of balance between these polarities.

The differences between men and women reflect the active and receptive principles at work in the universe, though those differences do not always have to dictate behavior patterns. Concepts of "male behavior" and "female behavior" are to some extent culturally dictated. On a spiritual level we are all both masculine and feminine in nature.

Culture and Gender Roles

Our cultural and personal definitions of "maleness" and "femaleness" are changing. In the past one hundred years we have witnessed a dramatic shift in traditional gender roles and identity, particularly within the Western world. It has wrought changes at the deepest levels of society and perhaps within the collective consciousness as well.

Those who are over the age of fifty or sixty can tell you that the male/female dynamic is a good bit different now than it was when they were growing up. I believe that the balancing of the yin and yang polarities in society and within individuals is a major evolutionary step towards planetary transformation.

In the last century we have broken out of many culturally defined limitations around what men and women can do, feel, say, think, and look like. Women can now hold positions of power. Men can act as care-givers. Women are moving towards equal rights in both the workplace and in the home. It is now more acceptable for men to express their feelings and to value their close male relationships. By taking on roles that were heretofore reserved for members of the opposite sex, the non-biological lines between male and female are now rather blurred.

These role changes are helping to shift the cultural programming of what men and women are "supposed" to be, and from these changes we learn that all of us can be nurturing and self-actualizing. This is a move towards balance within the self and within society.

The Cultural Origins of Gender Wounding

To begin to heal the traumas of gender, it is important to take a look at how we have been hurt by the limitations of gender role programming. Many of us have experienced gender wounding that has prevented us from living the full expression of our hopes and desires for our lives. Though every person has their own traumas and their resultant patterns, there are some basic themes that we can observe.

The Gender Wounding of Men

Very soon after birth, many men receive their first gender wounding, circumcision. This very painful surgery is routinely performed on many baby boys as if it is no big deal. Though if an adult man was asked to have a piece of skin cut off his penis without anesthesia, there is no way he would do it. Some people believe that babies don't really feel circumcision, but if you heard the screams a little baby makes at the time, it would be hard to deny that the child was experiencing intense pain. While the adult man may not consciously remember the event, the subconscious self most certainly does. Who knows what results this violence has on the child's psyche? Some people postulate that this early violation can lead to the man shutting down his capacity to feel and increases the likelihood of violence by men in society in general.[1]

As children, little boys are traditionally taught to shut down their ability to feel. They are told, "Big boys don't cry," "Stand up and take it like a man," and other damaging messages that lead them to believe that they are somehow deficient or weak if they have feelings or show vulnerability. Independence is praised, and dependence on others is discouraged.

Many boys do not receive the intimacy that they crave. Fathers often develop emotional distance from their children, often focusing their attention on professional successes instead. This lack of intimacy is perpetuated into adulthood as emotional intimacy between men is not encouraged and homophobia divides men still further.

From adolescence on, boys are expected and encouraged to compete and to succeed. In this achievement oriented society, competing and winning are predominant ways in which men get acknowledged and appreciated. Men are often consciously or unconsciously put in a position of watching out for, or trying to become, the "Alpha male." The Alpha male is either physically, psychologically, or socially in a position of power within a group. This dynamic reinforces the tendency towards hierarchical social structuring. Men learn to be wary of one another, which erodes much of their potential for deep trust. As a result, many men feel the need to cultivate the appearance of being self-assured, when in fact they may feel insecure. This pressure to achieve often leads men to wonder if they are "real men."

The focus on competition in our society drives men to push themselves unceasingly in order to prove their self-worth, extending into all aspects of a man's life including work and sexual conquest. When success is measured outwardly by comparing and competing with others, feelings of impotence and insecurity are unavoidable. A person can always find others who can excel beyond what has been personally achieved. Anger and resentment are feelings that are also prevalent as men's inner emotional needs go unmet. All these feelings lead some men towards acts of violence in order to feel powerful.

As a result of the competition and estrangement between men, women often become the only acceptable outlet for a man's need for intimacy, providing the caring denied them in their lives. This need is often expressed in sexual desire, as men sometimes experience sex as the only place in their lives they can get closeness. Deep down, many men feel a deep anger about this lack of intimacy and loneliness that they have experienced. This can lead a man to feel as though he is at the mercy of a woman's choice. Much of the sexual violence towards women is an expression of a man's anger about his inability to control his accessibility to intimacy and his feelings of powerlessness in a power-oriented society.

The Gender Wounding of Women

Women are traditionally taught from infancy to be passive and pliant. Little girls are often told to "Smile" and to "Be a good girl." Girls are especially praised for doing as they are told. The desire for approval becomes fixated on the desire to please other people, and this encourages them to aspire to servitude in order to be loved. Even in today's society where some women hold high paying jobs and positions of authority, they are often expected to clean the house, do the shopping, and take care of the children as well. In the western world, it can seem as though women have equality with men, but they still make less money than men in comparable jobs. The glass ceiling of gender privilege allows for the illusion of equality, yet true equality has still not been reached.

As children, girls generally receive a great deal of praise and scorn based on their physical appearance. They grow to believe that their looks are the basis of their self-worth. Early on, issues of weight and appearance become critical for many young women.

THE YIN AND YANG OF IT ALL

Women of all ages go to such extremes as starvation diets and bingeing and purging to reach some idealized physical appearance. Women often work out issues regarding repressed sexuality, fear, guilt, self-sabotage, self image through their relationship with food. For many women, food becomes a substitute for love. Women often go to extremes in regards to their physical body in order to keep in line with a stylized notion of what women "should" look like according to projected stereotypes of desirability. They way women are portrayed in the media and film industries has a strong impact on the self-esteem of many women by reinforcing notions of "an ideal woman."

All of this focus on physical appearance and ability to nurture gives girls the message that their worth is based on their ability to attract a mate and their ability to adapt to men's needs. Within this societal model, a woman's world revolves around the man, and her personal goals and needs are secondary. Worth is assessed in relation to partnership. Women wish to see their role of service as being an expression of their ability to be loving and nurturing rather than as a role of servitude and lack of decision making power in the destiny of their lives. This applies in women's careers as well as in relationships. Women in service-related jobs often focus more on their ability to serve others than on the fact that they are poorly paid or that their ideas are often co-opted by their superiors.

Women are conditioned to be sex objects through social interaction and the media. Images of sex are everywhere, selling all kinds of products. Women themselves appear to be products that can be bought or sold. Sexuality is at once glorified and reviled; moreover, women are encouraged to be sexually attractive in a sexually repressed society. Women are allowed and encouraged to have the outward trappings of being sexual, such as seductive clothing, but find that it can be socially unacceptable to manifest their sexual nature except within the narrow constructs of the societal norm. This creates a double standard in which a woman is considered desirable if she appears sexy but is stigmatized as a "bad girl" if she engages in sexual conduct outside the institution of marriage or relationship.

Violence against women is endemic in our society. Women are often subject to brutality. The traumas of incest, rape, and other forms of physical and emotional abuse make women feel powerless. Many women live with a constant fear of being abused. A woman cannot even walk down the street at night in the United States without fear. Every two and half minutes, someone in the US is sexually assaulted. Ninety percent of the time, that person is a woman. Statistics state that 1 in 6 women has been the victim of an attempted or completed rape. [2] This culture of violence serves to immobilize women, effectively maintaining the status quo of the current power structure.

There are many women who perceive themselves to be victims and do not know how to reclaim their power. Women are often afraid to speak their minds or act powerfully for fear of physical or emotional abuse. Often women resort to passive aggressive behaviors because they do not feel safe or justified in directly stating their needs or feelings.

Since women's value within this society is based primarily on youthful sexual attractiveness, older women are often disregarded. Our modern society has an infatuation with youthfulness. People go to great lengths to look young. The media advertising wants us to believe that signs of age are undesirable. This is particularly so for women. Older men are more likely to be considered "distinguished looking" with age. Women, on the other hand, lose their usefulness when they lose their youthful looks, because it is a women's body, not her wisdom that is considered to be her main attribute of desirability. As the grayness and wrinkles increase, many women find themselves faced with a growing feeling of invisibility. People begin to ignore and overlook them in all aspects of life in society.

The level of dysfunctionality that men and women experience within our society is still prevalent, but it is not hopeless. Being aware of the problems is the first step to transformation. In order to change to a model of society that is healthy and positive for both men and women, some basic shifts in perspective must be made.

Balancing Polarity Within Society

It is much easier to see how women and men have been wounded than it is to imagine what people would be like if issues around gender were healed. We do not have very many, if any, archetypes of healed male and female energy to draw from. To heal men and women, it will require not only healing male energy in men, and female energy in women, but it will require that women integrate healed masculine energy and men integrate healed feminine energy within themselves. A balance would need to be achieved within many individuals in order to create a larger societal healing. "Self-discovery inevitably involves the awakening of traits usually associated with the opposite sex. All the gifts of the human mind are available to the conscious self: nurturance and independence, sensitivity and strength. If we complete such qualities within ourselves, we are not as dependent on others for them. Much of what has been labeled love in our culture is infatuation with, and the need for, our missing halves."[3] By the development of our potential through internal gender balancing, the potential for humanity as a whole to become balanced may be realized.

The Anima and the Animus

Carl Jung, one of the pioneers in the field of human psychology, put a great emphasis on the anima and animus. The anima represents the female aspect within man, and the animus represents the masculine aspect within woman. The anima and animus represent the qualities we associate with being men and women. Making a conscious connection with these aspects of ourselves is one way to come into a more balanced place with our active and receptive aspects and to acknowledge our true nature as androgynous souls. The power of androgyny lies in rediscovering the opposites within one's self and in reintegrating the parts of ourselves that have been lost to us through societal sex-role behavioral training.

In order to positively recreate the masculine and feminine energies, we need some positive role models to work from. In the theater of our minds we can create opportunities for our wounded parts to heal and create archetypes as positive examples of maleness and femaleness. If you could create Divine archetypes of healed and whole masculinity and femininity, what would they be like? Perhaps, they would be like having Gods and Goddesses that would inhabit our own psyches.

The Goddess and God within represent an ultimate internal concept of healed masculine and feminine energy. Conceiving of both a God and a Goddess can require a hefty belief system shift for those who have been raised in monotheistic traditions. Many have little reference for a female representation of Divinity. On the other hand, there are many who have found connection with the Goddess and turned away from monotheistic view of God as male.

The Healing Archetypes

We can rewrite the script of how we perceive Divinity in order to create healing archetypes. The Goddess can be a powerful maiden, a sexual being, a nurturing mother, and the one who brings death that leads to transformation. The God can be strong and compassionate, playful and gentle, firm and kind, protecting as well as nurturing. He is the Sun of our conscious knowing. She is the Moon of our inner knowing. Together, they can help us to heal and transform the negative self concepts and limiting belief systems of our wounded selves.

When we are able to visualize archetypes of Divinity as both male and female, our ability to see Divinity within all is expanded. Both women and men need archetypes of Divinity to model after in order to remember wholeness. If we are to actualize power-sharing in society and in the relationship between the sexes, it makes sense to have power-sharing within the archetypes of our spiritual reality. In order to achieve inner balance, balancing the masculine and feminine polarities within ourselves is important.

The wounded male and female represent our negative self-concept in relation to our active and receptive natures. Observing them in the following visualization will help you to perceive how the wounding of your inner female and male has affected you. It may also reveal the overall concept of maleness and femaleness that you acquired from your life experience and from societal programming. In this visualization, you will also meet with the God and Goddess aspects that will represent your concept of healed and whole maleness and femaleness. Men and women are encouraged to do both meditations as men and women often require healing for both aspects.

Meditations on the Inner Male and Female:

Healing the Feminine

Take several breaths and allow yourself to relax. Imagine you are taking a path that goes off to your left from where you are lying. The path goes down a hill. You are on a sacred journey to meet the Goddess within, and to meet your wounded inner female. At the bottom of the hill is a temple dedicated to the feminine force. See the temple before you. Take in all the details. You are greeted at the door by the initiates of the temple. They bathe you and dress you in white. The women anoint you with beautiful smelling sacred oils that remind you of the Goddess. Breathe deeply and take in the pleasing fragrance.

You are blindfolded and led into the temple to meet your Goddess self. Prepare yourself to meet her. When the blindfold is removed, see her in front of you. Take time to really absorb all the details of how she looks. Notice her hair, her eyes, and how she is dressed. Pay attention to the way you feel in her presence. Embrace her, and feel the love that you share. Feel how your hearts connect. Look deeply into her eyes, taking in the depth of her being. Allow the healing force to flow into you from her. Shut your eyes, and feel yourself dissolving into space with her, becoming a part of the cosmic void energy. Allow all the holding and "tightness" in your body, mind, and emotions to dissolve, releasing your pain, fear, confusion, and dis-ease. Feel yourself merge with the vastness of space. Feel all space filled with the Divine force of love. Open your eyes in the vision, and thank the Goddess.

It is now time to meet with your wounded female self. Imagine you are walking down a hall towards the room where your wounded female self lives. You can look through a window and see her there. Pay attention to how she looks. How old is she? What position is she in? How does she hold her body? Does she look well? What do you think she is feeling? How is she dressed? When you are ready, enter the room. Does she acknowledge your presence? How do you think she feels about you? How do you feel about her?

Guide her out of the room she is in and walk towards the entry room of the Temple where you met your Goddess self. Before you enter the room, the initiates of the temple bathe, dress, and anoint her. Bring your wounded female self into the room to meet with your Goddess self. See her being held by the Goddess. Ask your wounded female what she needs in order to be healed. Do whatever you can to make her feel safe and cared for. Think of things you could do now and in your life that can help her to heal. Experience both the Goddess and yourself healing this part of yourself. See and feel her transforming before your eyes.

It is time to leave the temple. Know that you can return at any time. Walk back the way you came and re-enter your resting body from the left side. Be aware of sensations within your body. Feel your self being fully present in your body awareness.

Healing the Masculine

Shut your eyes again and imagine you are taking a path that goes off to your right from where you are lying. The path goes up a hill. You are on a sacred journey to meet the God within and your wounded inner male. At the top of the hill is a temple dedicated to the masculine energy. See the temple before you. Take in all the details. You are greeted at the door by the initiates of the temple. They burn sacred herbs, which they fan over you to purify you in preparation to meet the God within. Breathe deeply and take in the fragrance. You are dressed in white. A blindfold is placed over your eyes, and you are led into the temple to meet your God self. Prepare yourself to meet him. When the blindfold is removed, see him in front of you.

Take time to really absorb all the details of how he looks. Notice his hair, his eyes, and how he is dressed. Pay attention to the way you feel in his presence. Embrace him, and feel the love between you. Feel how your hearts connect, experiencing his gentleness and his power. Look deeply into his eyes, taking in the depth of his being. Allow the healing force to flow into you from him. Experience the spark of life that he represents. See that you are both being enveloped in a giant healing flame of white light. Feel your awareness growing stronger by the moment. Feel energy running through your body, healing and transforming your entire being. Become the flame of white light. Open your eyes and thank the God.

It is now time to meet with your wounded male self. Imagine you are walking down a hall towards the room where your wounded male self resides. You can look through a window and see him there. Pay attention to how he looks. How old is he? What position is he in? How does he hold his body? Does he look well? What do you think he is feeling? How is he dressed? When you are ready, enter the room. Does he acknowledge your presence? How do you think he feels about you? How do you feel about him?

Guide him out of the room towards the entry room of the Temple where you met your God self. Before you enter the room, the initiates of the temple purify him with incense and dress him. Now bring him into the room to meet with your God self. See him as being held by God. Ask your wounded male what he needs to be healed. Do whatever you can to make him feel safe and cared for. Figure out things you could do within this visualization and in your life that can help him to heal. Experience both God and yourself healing your wounded male. See how he is transformed.

It is time to leave the temple. Know that you can return at any time. Walk back the way you came and re-enter your resting body from the right side. Be aware of your body. Open your eyes and become aware of your surroundings again.

How All of this Affects our Relationships

Carl Jung perceived the idea of the inner consort as an aspect of the self that is represented by a set of behaviors and characteristics. He called these two parts the anima (the feminine aspect of man) and the animus (the masculine aspect of a woman). Jung considered the anima or animus to represent our idealized partner. When we find someone we idealize as the ideal partner, we tend to project our own idealized opposite onto that person. After the initial glow wears off and reality sets in, we get to find out who that person actually is, instead of whom we have projected onto them.

Endings of relationships can often be devastating. Partially, it is because of the very real loss of that person, and sometimes it is because of our perceived loss of an ideal. When we project our anima or animus onto another person, we run the risk of temporarily losing a part of ourselves. If we can realize our ideal partner always lives within us, it can help us to be happy no matter what is going on in or out of relationship.

Sweet Mystery of Life, at Last I've Found You!
or:
Whoops, I'm with Someone
like Daddy (or Mommy) Again!

Dr. Harville Hendrix came up with great relationship theory called the "Imago match." The imago match is a person that you would be likely to choose because that person fits your psychological profile perfectly. Your *Imago*, which is a Latin term for *image*, is essentially a composite picture of the people who most influenced you at an early age. Dr. Hendrix believes that you unconsciously choose a partner, an *Imago match*, who has positive and negative traits similar to your parents. This partner has the potential to help you heal unresolved pain from childhood.[4]

Your imago match is likely to be similar to your mother or father in some significant positive and negative ways. By being with this person, you would find your core material would be stimulated. That activation of material could help you to work out unresolved issues from childhood. However, it can sometimes make issues worse if you do not work with it consciously. For instance, if a woman had a father who was a workaholic and was emotionally unavailable, she would be very likely to end up with someone who had similar tendencies. The funny thing I've noticed about this is that even if a person is determined to choose someone who does not have the negative aspects of mom, dad, or their last partner, nine times out of ten, that new person will end up having similar characteristics even though they appeared to be different in the beginning. It just goes to show you, wherever you go, your stuff goes with you.

It has been my experience that as we work out our own personal issues, the level of our ability to manifest healed partnership gets much stronger. Instead of falling madly in love with someone who pushes all of our buttons, we heal the buttons. Then we are free to choose someone, or we are free to view our current love as being more like our ideal inner consort.

Tantra, Polarity, and Sexuality

Let's face it; sex is a touchy subject (pun intended). Some people think sex is heaven. Some believe sex is a sin. Some believe sex is a sin in some cases. Others don't believe in sin. Some believe in monogamy, some believe in polyamory. Some people don't believe in marriage. Some people believe homosexuality is evil; others believe homosexuality is the best thing since apple pie. Sexuality is an arena in which people often have very strong opinions. Sexual drive is a physical expression of the life force energy. We cannot help but feel strongly about it because its influence touches the core of our energetic self.

According to some tantric texts, nothing is forbidden. In *Left-handed* or *Red Tantra,* everything is seen as sacred. Nothing is judged as good or bad. Every experience is an opportunity to learn that there is no division. We are not separating people, things and behaviors into good and bad; we are not dividing the world into right or wrong. Both pleasant and unpleasant experiences are opportunities for us to grow. When we embrace all things, our capacity to love, to enjoy life, and to be ecstatic becomes stronger because we are not rejecting reality or rejecting aspects of our experience.

The word tantra is derived from two root words. "Tan" comes from *tanoti,* which means expansion. "Tra" is derived from *trayati*, with means liberation. Through tantra, we are given tools to expand our consciousness and weave our perception of all creation as limitless and indivisible as the Divine experience. This expansion liberates our energy, increasing our potential on every level.[5]

In addition to the biological necessity of procreation, the sexual urge is born of the desire to merge with another person and ultimately with the universe in an ecstatic way. Tantra is a spiritual path that assists in the balancing and merging of the polarities.

Tantra is a word that describes a multitude of beliefs, practices and spiritual lineages. For many people, the word *tantra* has to do with the merging of sexuality and spirituality, though there are many Tantric traditions that do not work with physical sexual energy. The perception by Westerners that tantra is about peak sexual experience is an extreme simplification. Within the sexual arena, tantric practice can create opportunities for healing and enlightenment as well as profoundly enhance the sexual experience.

Sexual tantric practice can be a way to reclaim the sacredness of sexuality and the body. It is a means to balance the yin and yang energies and clear the energetic system of blockages. It is a way to become more intimate and connected with one's partner. Sex is a sacred act. It is a physical and emotional manifestation of the universe's natural quest for balance and completion. One of the esoteric reasons we choose to come into relationship with other people is because they represent the part of us that we need to integrate. They are mirrors for how we need to grow and evolve to be complete within ourselves.

Some people choose celibacy over relationship in order to completely merge internally without external distractions. Neither the path of relationship, nor the path of celibacy, is inherently more merit-filled than another. Each has its inherent lessons, benefits, and challenges.

Tantra and Androgyny

To balance the active and receptive principles through the path of relationship, it is not necessary to be in a heterosexual relationship. The true nature of the yin and yang principles is not indicated by physical form. All people are a balance of the two polarities. Any person of either sex can be a mirror for growth.

For that matter, men do not always primarily exhibit the male polarity and women do not always primarily exhibit female polarity tendencies. It is not unusual for a man to be receptive, nurturing and empathic or for a woman to be protective, assertive and analytical. Either may be prevalent.

Ideally, we are in a balance between the polarities. By balancing our inner polarities, we can learn how to use the power and energy these polarities contain to respond to life appropriately in the way that serves us best. When the characteristics are balanced, we have the skills and energy inherent in the polarities available to us, so we can respond appropriately when those characteristics are needed.

In Hindu Tantrism, the polarities become reversed. The feminine energy becomes more active in nature and the masculine energy expresses the stillness of awakened awareness. This basic shift is like the black dot in the white field of the yin-yang symbol: it is the essence of the opposite polarity within each side of the yin-yang, which creates stability and harmonious flow between the polarities.

Ida and Pingala

Ida and *pingala* are two energetic channels, or nadis in the body, as described by Vedic energetic anatomy. Ida and pingala spiral around the spinal nadi called the shushumna, appearing very much like the double helix of our DNA. The two energy channels cross each other at each of the energetic chakra vortexes. The shushumna, ida, and pingala nadis all meet at the ajna chakra midway between the eyebrows. A familiar symbol that represents the flow of these three channels is the caduceus, which was adopted as a symbol of western medicine a century ago. These channels are considered to be the three main highways towards awakened kundalini and enlightenment. The ida and pingala channels relate to our dual nature. It is believed that when they are in perfect balance, the center or shushumna channel awakens,  bringing us to enlightenment. This is apparent in the meaning of the word *hatha* of hatha yoga. In Sanskrit, "ha" and "tha" are two mantras. 'Ha' represents the vital solar force of pingala, and 'Tha' represents the lunar qualities of ida.

The ida channel begins and ends on the left side of the body. The energy that runs through the channel is considered lunar, cool and nurturing by nature. It represents the more feminine aspects of our personality. Within the pingala channel travels the solar energy, which begins and ends on the right side of the spine. It is warm and stimulating by nature and oversees the masculine aspects of our personality. The interaction between these channels directly relates to the relationship between energy and consciousness, intuition and rationality, and the functioning of the right and left brain hemispheres.

Throughout the day, one or the other channel is dominant. Those changes are determined by our tendencies of personality, behavior and health. Most people tend towards either ida tendencies or pingala tendencies. People whose strength is in ida will have a tendency towards lunar qualities but may lack the ability to direct energy and action. People with strong pingala tendencies are likely to have lots of creativity and vitality but may lack the introspection and receptivity necessary for peace and spiritual awakening.

When ida and pingala are perfectly balanced, it causes the *prana*, or life force, to flow evenly so that the central shushumna channel can then open awakening sublime awareness. The balance of these channels is like a marriage. It is the wedding of the sun and the moon, the night and the day. In Sanskrit, this wedding is called *sandhya* and this marriage is a cause for happiness. All of the self becomes joined in union, merging self to self, joining together as a manifestation of the Divine being.

Nadi Shodhana

Nadi Shodhana is a meditative practice that assists the ida and pingala channels to come into perfect balance. It also assists in the purification of the energetic system. To begin, block the right nostril and breath in and out of the left nostril several times, giving an equal amount of time to the inhalation and exhalation. Repeat the process by blocking the left nostril and breathing in and out of the right nostril. This is the first level of the Nadi Shodhana practice. By doing this, you can discover whether ida on the left or pingala on the right is currently dominant. You might consider checking your nostrils throughout the day to see which one is dominant more often. You also might notice whether the flows are coming into balance if you practice Nadi Shodhana regularly.

To perform Nadi Shodhana, place your right index finger and middle finger on your third eye. Allow your thumb and ring finger to hover over either nostril. Place your tongue on the roof of your mouth at the indentation in the palate a little ways behind the teeth. Press the right nostril in, blocking the flow of air. Draw energy and air in through the left nostril and imagine you are drawing that energy up to the third eye in the form of light. Close both nostrils and hold your attention at the third eye while you hold your breath. Release the right nostril and allow the air to escape out of it. At the same time, imagine energy flowing down the right side of your body. On your next inhalation, draw the air in through the right nostril up to the third eye. Close both nostrils and hold your attention and the energy at the third eye. Open the left nostril and allow the energy to flow down the left side of your body. Repeat this process by drawing the energy up the left side of the body up to the third eye and so on, so forth. This will help to balance the ida and pingala channels and still the mind.

3

The Power of the Trinity

The Triquetra symbol represents the 'Power of Three' or the threefold nature of existence. The triad can represent the entirety of a cycle, as it contains a beginning, middle and an end, which similarly represents the cycle of birth, life and death. It also represents the three times: past, present  and future. There are three cycles of the moon: waxing, full and waning. It can represent the body, mind and spirit; the Sun, the Moon, and the Earth; and the creative process of thought, word, and deed. To the mathematician Pythagoras, 3 represented the number of completion. The power of three is often considered to represent the powerful structure of the indissoluble unity of creation.

Spiritual mythology is filled with sacred trinities. The ancient Greeks had the sacred trinity of Kore, Demeter, and Hecate. Christians worship the Father, the Son, and Holy Ghost. Hindus worship the three cosmic couples: Brahma and Saraswati, Vishnu and Lakshmi, and Kali and Shiva. The ancient Celts and Greeks honored the trinity of the Goddess as Maiden, Mother, and Crone.

Within the strength of the cycle there is unlimited potential for creation through the power of multiplicity. In 1 we have the essence and all that is, in 2 we have the union, and 3 represents the children of that union, which is all possibility.

The Threefold Levels of Consciousness

In *transpersonal psychology*, the three selves are defined as the conscious, subconscious and the super-conscious selves. The conscious self deals with our linear perception of reality while in an awakened state. The subconscious mind is the subterranean part of the self that functions in the background processing information and holding memory. The super-conscious self is the aspect of self that is aware of the larger patterns of life and the soul's interaction with those patterns.

There is an interestingly parallel relationship between transpersonal psychology and the Hawaiian Kahuna tradition's concept of the self. Both systems view the self as having three parts that are in constant interaction with one another.

The concept of the triune self is essential to Kahuna philosophy. Within the Kahuna system, the self is composed of three basic parts: the low self (unihipili), the middle self (uhane), and the high self (aumakua). Each part of the self has different skills and needs, which are similar to those of transperonal psychology. Each plays a different role within the totality of the self. In Kahuna healing, working with the relationship between the three selves is one of the core means of accessing healing, wisdom, spiritual growth and emotional growth. Let's take a look at these three parts from the Kahuna perspective.

The Low Self

The low self, or subconscious mind, is the body mind. Practitioners within the Kahuna tradition call this part of the self

THE POWER OF THE TRINITY   45

the "*unihipili*." It is the etheric body, which is the light body double of your physical body. The solar plexus is the focal point of this aspect of the self. The unihipili is responsible for creating, recreating, and maintaining the physical body. It has natural needs that relate to the physical needs of the body (food, water, protection and sex). It is the part that keeps you breathing even when you are not thinking about breathing, keeps your heart pumping, and regulates the functioning of your organs, nerves, tissues, bones and glands. In short, it keeps your physical boat afloat. It can be thought of as the animal aspect of self. It is in direct contact with the natural world. The unihipili is also responsible for storing and categorizing all memories, beliefs, and programming you receive in your life. The low self only stores these memories, beliefs and programs; it does not create them.

The Middle Self

The middle self, conscious mind, or the *uhane*, is responsible for the retrieval of information from both intellectual and intuitive sources. It analyzes and integrates the experiences of your life and forms beliefs, opinions, and attitudes based on the information that the low self already holds. Upon this, it makes decisions that help to direct your life's course. The uhane is also the source of your will. Its center is located in the brain. The middle self gathers both thoughts and feelings and sends them to the low self to be stored. The uhane can be thought of as your ego self. The middle self has personal and social needs and relates to the needs of the ego. The middle self needs to be recognized, to be respected and to receive attention. It needs admiration and seeks status and appreciation from others in order to gain self-esteem. The middle self also needs relationship in order to feel complete.

The uhane is your astral body, which has the ability to travel in ordinary reality within the vehicle of your body, and in the non-ordinary reality of the spirit world through astral travel and shamanic journeying to retrieve information not so readily available in the ordinary reality of the third dimension.

The High Self

The high self, super-conscious mind, or the *aumakua* is the part of the self that is fully enlightened. It guides and helps the conscious and subconscious selves to know, love and connect with the Divine in all things. The high self seeks the higher attributes, including the needs for Truth, Love, Beauty, Wisdom and Peace. Its job is to give gentle, non-judgmental support and unconditional love. It is your teacher self, and it can be counted on to provide wisdom and guidance on what is best for you and your path in life. Often this guidance is given through dreams. [1]

The Threefold Relationship

The centerpiece of working with these three different parts of the self is the development of clear communication between the selves so that the whole self can be healed and transformed. Serge Kahili King has a lovely little analogy for the three selves, relating to them as if they are three beings that live on three different floors of a house. The high self lives in the attic. It can look out its windows and have a grand overview of the yard, the trees, and the surrounding areas. From this perspective it can see the greater relationship of things and their place in the world.

The middle self lives on the first floor. The middle self has a view, but that view is obstructed by trees, fences, and other houses. These obstructions could be likened to our filters or perceptions that color our view of reality. Because of those obstructions, the middle self, or conscious mind, only sees a small portion of the true nature of reality.

The low self lives in the basement and has no external view on reality. It is totally reliant on the other two selves for a view of what lies beyond the confines of the house. All its information is second-hand. It can't tell the difference between a real life experience and a movie. Even though its view is completely dependent on the other two parts, it has a very important job. It stores all the mind's thoughts and the reactions of the emotions in the basement vault.[2]

According to Kahuna philosophy, the interplay between these three parts is of critical importance. The conscious mind, or middle self, on the first floor cannot directly interface with the super-conscious mind, or the higher self on the top floor. The conscious mind can only interact with the super-conscious mind through the subconscious, or low self, in the basement. Even though the unihipili is referred to as the "low self," *low* does not mean *less*. Working with the unihipili is the key to all our dreams, needs, and aspirations. Without the cooperation of the unihipili, we can do nothing.

For example, let's say you created an affirmation for yourself, like, "I deserve love." You can say it as much as you want, but until you are able to experience the concept as a living experience in the form of body knowledge or sensation; it will remain an idea instead of a fully realized phenomenon. Since the low self is the repository of beliefs, emotions and experiences that are held in the body, the concept will be reflected by positive sensation in the body only when the knowledge or affirmation has been fully integrated into the subconscious. When the blockages and low self-esteem are purified from the low self, the light of the high self can then penetrate through all levels of the self to bring about the desired transformation. Once a person is able to take something from the realm of idea and integrate it into the deepest part of the psyche, then the combined selves are able to manifest that affirmation as a living reality. The centerpiece of working with these three different parts of the self is to develop clear communication between the selves so that the whole self can be healed and transformed.

All our physical sensations and perceptions are felt by the unihipili and are relayed to the conscious mind to be met with actions or reactions. Pain is a good example of a common way the subconscious communicates with the conscious mind through sensation. "Ouch! It's time to move the finger off the stove." An example of an unconscious reaction to ingrained programming might be that every time you smell Chanel No.5, on a subconscious level you are reminded of your Aunt Matilda, whom you don't like. Your immediate reaction is a strong desire to run upstairs and hide in the closet when you smell that perfume. Ideally, we can learn how to respond to the perceptions of our environment appropriately but not be in reaction to old programming held in the subconscious self that does not serve us any longer.

This is why hypnotherapy is so effective. In hypnotherapy, the subconscious mind is fed suggestions, which can help to transform sensory perceptions and beliefs about the nature of reality and the nature of the self. When the subconscious mind accepts these suggestions as true, the body mind digests that information. Once those concepts are integrated, profound changes are possible. Contrary to superstitions about hypnotism, no one can be hypnotized to do or believe something they don't want to do or believe. All hypnosis is a form of self-hypnosis. With the approval of the conscious mind, the subconscious mind can receive the suggestion. With the assistance of the high self, apparent miracles of healing are possible. An operation can be performed without pain, an old habit can be broken, or a phobia can be released.

Meditations on the Three Selves

In this meditation, you will be traveling into the three worlds to meet with your three selves. Lie down in a comfortable position in a place you will not be interrupted. Take three deep breaths, and release them with a sigh. With each breath, you become more and more relaxed. Be aware of each part of your body in turn, observing the sensations in each place. Start at your toes and move up to your head, relaxing each part as you pay attention to it. Remember to breathe deeply as you move your consciousness through your body.

You are now walking across a flat field towards a house. Imagine that within the house is your conscious self. Walk up to the door and enter. You see and feel your conscious self before you. Look carefully at this being and its surroundings. Take time to perceive the inner workings of this being as an observer. What are the motivating desires, patterns, tendencies and goals that drive this being? Look deeply into the eyes of your conscious self. What do you see? Pay attention to details so you can recall them later. Ask this part of your self what it needs to feel fulfilled and healed. Embrace this being and feel yourself merge with your conscious self. Examine how you and your body feel being fully merged with your conscious self. Thank your conscious self.

When you are ready, leave the house and journey down a long hill that winds down into a deep forest. At the bottom of the hill is the house of your subconscious self. Take in the details of the house before you enter. As you enter, experience this part of yourself in whatever form it comes to you, whether it is a person or animal, a child or an adult, form or formless. Bring all of your senses into play. Feel, see, hear, smell, and perhaps even taste the experience of being in the home of your subconscious self. Also take some time to be aware of this being's surroundings. Take some time to observe this part of your self. What does this part seem to be feeling? How do you feel about this part of your self? Do you appreciate it, or does it make you uncomfortable in some way? Try to feel what this being needs. Can you promise to fulfill these needs? Embrace it and shower it with love, affection, and appreciation. This part of you really needs all the positive reinforcement you can give. Tell it how much you appreciate all the good work it does. Let it know that you would like to stay in clear contact with it. Let this part of you know that you will do your best to not say bad things about your self any more. Ask this part of yourself what it would like to be called, or give this subconscious part of you a name.

Share with your subconscious self the needs conveyed to you by your conscious self. Ask it to help manifest these things for you. When you ask, play the needs by like a movie in which you see your true needs being fulfilled, as if it is happening in present time. Feel it in your body and with your emotions as well as seeing it in your mind's eye. See that movie of needs and desires in a magical bubble that floats between you. Imagine that you are both charging the manifestation with cosmic energy. When the energy starts to peak, both of you step forward and merge into the bubble and into each other. Allow the merging to be complete. Thank your subconscious self, and leave the house.

You are now walking up the hill. You come to a tall mountain and you begin to climb. Feel the air around you get crisper and cleaner as you ascend. You feel a sense of expectancy and excitement about meeting this enlightened part of your self. As you walk on the path up the mountain, you feel as though you are growing lighter with every step. When you reach the top of the mountain, see your high self coming to meet you. Feel the energy of pure unconditional love flow to you from your high self. See the wisdom and beauty of the Divine in this being's eyes. Lie down on top of the mountain and feel your high self healing you with the love and the light of universal life force energy. Feel the healing energy pour into your body, your heart, and your mind. Allow joy and bliss to fill you. Breathe deeply and let the healing energy into every cell of your body. Really enjoy it. Take some time to integrate these healing energies.

Now, sit up and look into the eyes of your high self. Ask your high self to share with you the wisdom you need right now in your life. Really take in the message given. Share with your high self your vision bubble of fulfillment. Ask her/him for blessings upon the vision and help in manifesting it in a way that honors the highest good for yourself and all beings. Place the bubble between you. Feel your high self charging the bubble with very powerful life force energy. Feel yourself filling with confidence and joy, fulfillment and ease. See the bubble rising into the sky like a cloud as you merge into your high self. Feel a gentle rain of your vision sprinkling down on you, becoming manifest in your life. Thank your high self.

It is time to leave the mountain. You may return here whenever you wish. Have fun flying down the mountain and back into your body, here in this room. Breathe deeply. Feel the sensations of your body. Return to everyday consciousness when you are ready.

Shamanic Practices of the Three Worlds

What is Shamanism?

All over the world there are cultures of people who practice shamanism. The word *shaman* originates from the Tungus people of Siberia. Even though there are many different shamanic traditions in the world with different ceremonies, they share many similar beliefs about the nature of reality. *Shamanism* has become a word commonly used to describe spiritual belief systems in which the practitioner believes that all things of nature have life and consciousness. Every rock and plant has wisdom and a purpose. The planets, the sun, and the moon are thought of as conscious beings with their own intelligence. Shamans believe that all things are intrinsically connected through the web of life.

There are Shamans and medicine men and women who are still practicing their traditional rites in indigenous cultures throughout the world including, but not limited to, the Americas, Norway, Siberia, Mongolia, Lapland, Indonesia, Australia, Hawaii, Tibet, Nepal, Korea, and Africa. Once upon a time, the traditional cultures of Europe also had many shamanic practitioners. However, when Christianity came along, much of what was called Shamanism began to be called Witchcraft and its practices banned. These days, there is a revival of European shamanic traditions, some of which are based on what small fragments still remain from ancestral culture and some of which have been re-created by observing the shamanic traditions that are still alive on the planet. In addition, some of the shamanic practices and knowledge that are coming into common usage are based in people's firsthand experiences that have naturally arisen from personal experience of the three worlds and the wisdom inherent in nature.

A shaman is a person who can travel by means of their consciousness between ordinary and non-ordinary reality in order to receive wisdom and offer healing in service of their community. Ordinary reality is our everyday way of perceiving reality in our usual state of consciousness. Ordinary reality follows the laws of logic. Non-ordinary reality refers to a dimension or state of consciousness that the shaman travels into for healing and wisdom. Unlike ordinary reality, non-ordinary reality does not follow the rules of logic but is primarily based in the realm of symbol, metaphor and the cosmic relationship between all things.

Generally speaking, Shaman is a title that is given by a community and not a title that one self-proclaims. There are many people who practice shamanism, however, there are very few shamans. The title of shaman connotes a level of initiation and experience that goes beyond the average practitioner.

A common concept in the shamanic framework is the notion of the Three Worlds. These three worlds are three different dimensional realities. Each of these worlds contains different beings with whom the shaman can interact in order to facilitate healing and transformation.

The Shaman's Drum and Shamanic Journeying

Shamanic practitioners experience the three worlds by shamanic journeying. One of the most common ways to make a shamanic journey is through the use of the drum as a vehicle to transport the consciousness into non-ordinary reality. The drum beat helps the practitioner maintain focus as her/his astral body travels in different dimensional realms. The drum is beaten in a monotonous rhythm that helps the practitioner along on her/his journey. The drum is sometimes metaphorically referred to as the horse on which the shaman rides through the three worlds. It helps create a connection between ordinary and non-ordinary reality and the astral and physical body, making it easier to return back to the body after the journey is completed. This monotonous rhythm also helps to create an altered state of consciousness that

helps the shamanic practitioner to perceive non-ordinary reality more clearly. With modern day knowledge of brain waves, we now know that the speed of the rhythm often used in shamanic journeying helps to put the practitioner in the theta brain wave state, which facilitates the altered state of consciousness that is required for the journey.

For example, when the shamanic practitioner wishes to journey to the lower realms, the person would first imagine an entry way to the underworld. That might be a hole in the ground or in a tree, or that person could imagine walking down a hill or diving into water. The basic notion is to head downward. After a short transitionary period of moving from the ordinary reality to the underworld, the practitioner imagines that s/he comes out into another realm. This realm often looks much like the earthly realm. Then the practitioner traverses across this landscape and experiences whatever there is to be experienced. After a time, the practitioner will review all the experiences in the journey by retracing the steps of the journey. Then s/he will return to normal consciousness, bringing with them whatever knowledge or beneficial energies they might have encountered along the way.

For those just beginning, the shamanic journey can feel and seem as though it is just imagination gone wild. But really, inside the word "imagination" is the word "magi" which means "The Magicians." Our imagination is our best magical tool. Imagination is the key to opening and awakening ourselves on psychic and spiritual levels.

The shamanic journey is performed by the non-linear functions of the brain and of the psyche. Because the right brain controls the imaginative functions, the journey seems just like imagination. People get too concerned about whether or not something is "real" or not. Fixation on the need for empirical proof in order to have faith can deter spiritual and psychic development by undermining the process of opening to new possibilities.

The concern is not so much whether or not what is occurring is real. The point is to understand that the psyche is giving you a message, and to learn how to de-code that message. Our psyche speaks in the language of dreams, which is symbolism. By working with the symbols the psyche presents, we are given the key to contact the subconscious self, and through that contact, access the real powers that lie dormant within us. As a shamanic practitioner becomes more advanced, the symbols and the information that arise from journeying become more tangible and have a more tangible effect on the waking consciousness of both the practitioner and anyone else who they might journey for.

The Underworld

The lower world or the underworld, not to be confused with "hell," contains the involutionary energies. *Involutionary energies* are beings that relate directly to the natural world. The involutionary energies are represented by things that we interact with in the natural world, such as animals, plants, rocks and the elemental forces of air, fire, water and earth. From a shamanic perspective, all things have consciousness, even inanimate objects such as rocks. Shamans work with these involutionary energies and believe that everything can be communicated with if approached properly.

Animal Allies

Animal Allies are being that are found in the underworld. Most people who have been exposed to shamanism have heard of working with totems or animal allies. I think most people instinctively feel an emotional if not spiritual bond to animals. In shamanic traditions, when a spiritual connection is made to an animal ally, that connection goes beyond simple affinity and moves into a dynamic relationship that can bring about powerful positive change for the practitioner.

The animal allies provide information that can help us to see our own nature as well as provide protection both in the spiritual realms and in our worldly life. Having conscious contact with an animal ally is especially helpful for people who are interested in doing healing, divining, or other magical or psychically oriented work. It is important to have access to awareness on other dimensional levels in order to be protected and guided while practicing your craft. The ally can provide contact to that protection and awareness. In this way, your attention does not have to be split between focuses. The ally can perform one of these duties for you.

Each person has a different animal ally that works with him or her. Sometimes people have more than one ally. For some people, it is readily apparent what that animal is, and for others it may be unclear. The nature of the ally that chooses to work with you relates to something in your own nature you are working on. The shamanic practitioner can get in touch with that animal by shamanic journeying.

What Else is in the Underworld?

The lower realm is also populated by the little people. Some traditions call them fairies, elves, gnomes, and dwarves. They go by many names and are widely experienced by nature based traditions that practice shamanism. These beings are less dense than humans, comprised more of light and electromagnetic current than matter. Their job is to assist the essences of the Earth spirits to organize, pattern, and evolve creation. The fey do not have free will like humans. They serve the pattern that harmonizes nature.

Other energies and entities that can be contacted in the underworld are the spirits of the rocks, the spirits of the plants, the over lighting spirits of nature (also known as the devas,) and the elemental forces, which we will be discussing in Chapter 4.

The involutionary energies found in the underworld are concerned primarily with the *cosmic map*. The cosmic map is the organizational principle that, when followed helps all things planetary fit together perfectly in a harmonically functioning way. This map could be considered a blueprint. The beings within the involutionary construct do not have free will; they live completely in service to the map. When we consciously work in conjunction with the involutionary beings, we can apply the power of our free will to carrying out the plan according to the map and thus live in greater harmony within this planetary sphere.[3]

The Upper World

The upper world is populated by the *evolutionary energies*. These beings and states of being relate to our capacity for transformation on the highest level. The upper world energies consist of very fine vibrations above and beyond the dense and slow vibrations of the earthly realm. Some of those beings would include spirit guides, the archetypal energies, angels, enlightened masters out of body, deities, and some tribes of the star beings. These beings can offer us guidance and wisdom that takes us beyond where we have been to a new level of consciousness so that we may act in the world from a more enlightened perspective.

Through our many lifetimes, we have made connections and associations with different beings in the upper world. These connections can originate from different religious traditions that we have been a part of or from other interactions that we have had outside of religious constructs. For example, someone who has been raised in the Catholic Church may feel a profound connection to Mother Mary or the angelic realm. Someone who was raised as a Hindu might feel a profound connection to the elephant god Ganesh.

Some of these connections can remain active throughout our various lifetimes, and some of these connections go dormant because of particular beliefs we are having in a particular lifetime. This is not unlike old friends with whom we have lost contact because we are not interacting with them often. If a person is able to maintain an open mind, it is possible to reconnect with beings that we have interacted with in the past and reestablish connections. The *involutionary energies* attempt to maintain patterns that are healthy, whereas the *evolutionary energies* can jump the pattern to the next level of evolution. Evolutionary energies have choice, whereas the involutionary energies found in the lower world have not chosen free will; they have chosen to maintain the patterns.

In journeys to the upper world beings, the practitioner imagines going up into a realm above the physical realm. In this realm, the practitioner might receive a gift of energy or information that can help transform that person's life or the life of the person they are attempting to help. The information received in the upper realm often relates more to the journey of the soul beyond the current persona. From the perspective of the upper realm, we can see a broader view of the interconnections that make up the intricacy of life and our relationship to it. That perspective can give us insight to the greater karmic patterns at play. With this information, it is easier for us to make good choices that affect our well-being in the broadest sense. When the practitioner's consciousness returns to her/his body, s/he can bring back this gift that can help to change their own or someone else's perspective in order to bring about positive change.

The Middle World

The middle world is our ordinary reality, viewed from a non-ordinary or shamanic perspective. The middle world journey is a journey of the astral body in this physical dimension. In the journey, this can mean moving from one location to another, journeying through time, journeying within the practitioner's own body, or journeying in a client's body for healing and a greater understanding of the self.

Middle world journeying is related very directly to third dimensional existence. In a middle world journey, spiritual healing of the energy body can done that can help to change our physical, emotional, mental and psychic well-being. A person can also perform distance healing through a middle world journey. It is possible for a person to connect with another person anywhere on the planet. In the journey s/he can examine the patient and perform vibrational or shamanic healing and then return his or her consciousness to the physical body.

According to the philosophy of reincarnation, we live many lives and come back again and again in order to further our growth and complete karma. The middle world is the realm in which all our selves through space and time exist and can potentially interact. Our soul exists beyond time. All of these personas and their relative incarnations are just aspects of that totality. Through the middle world journey, the practitioner can gain a deeper knowledge of the total self and thus reclaim power lost in the past in order to create more powerful changes in the present and future.

The Spirits of the Dead

The middle world is also inhabited by states of being and non-corporeal entities that affect our health and well-being. This includes the spirits of the dead. Talking to spirits of the dead through Ouija boards, automatic writing, and channeling became popularized in western society through spiritualist and occult traditions. While  this can be a fascinating pastime, spirits of the dead do not always have correct information or an enlightened perspective, so the information is not always all that accurate. Probably, the most common and useful application of speaking to the dead is contacting loved ones who have passed over to the other side. This can help to alleviate some of the feelings of loss and grief that those left behind usually feel.

People who have passed over often can come back to check in on loved ones and relatives if the belief system they held in life would have allowed for the possibility of them doing it. People who believed that spirit communication was "evil" are less likely to come back and visit because what we believe dictates our reality. However, some of those people are able to grasp a larger perspective soon after death and eventually gain the ability to visit the living if they are able to stretch their concept of reality enough to encompass it.

Some people who have passed on get stuck between the worlds because they died suddenly and feel as though they are incomplete with their last incarnation. These people do not necessarily have negative intent towards the living but they exist in a state of mental and emotional confusion that they do not know how to get themselves out of.

There are some beings that have not moved on to other the other plane and are trapped between the worlds. They are ghosts in limbo. Often, they are confused and lost, or they are hanging around third dimensional reality trying to find entry into our dimension. I have heard many stories of how alcoholics who have passed on still hang around bars wishing for one more drink.

Speaking to the dead is not without its risks. Sometimes spirits of the dead hang around the world of the living in order to try to get a foothold back in through the back-door and in so doing cause some problems for those who attempt to communicate with them.

Shaman as Psycho-Pomp

One of the roles a shaman can play is to help assist souls that have passed on but are caught between the worlds. They are not able to come back into our dimension, but for some reason, they also have not been able to move on. The shaman in this case could be called a *psycho pomp*. One technique a psycho pomp might use would be to connect the being with other non-corporeal entities that can show him or her the way through positive encouragement and assist the spirit to resolve any anxieties about moving on to the other side. It is a kind of psychotherapy for the dead, if you will.

I remember an occasion once where I was in a haunted house and came across a spirit who was unable to pass to the other side. He had a great fear of going beyond the state of limbo because he believed that he had been such a bad person in his life and that he was bound to go to hell. While a concept of hell may be very real for some people, I do not subscribe to the notion of eternal damnation. I believe that all beings can eventually attain enlightenment. My encouragement to him was to know that the Divine Being loves and accepts him no matter what he has done. Through that divine forgiveness and the application of awareness to his choices, it would be possible for him to not only gain access to the heavenly realms but also to move beyond his current state of misery towards some sort of inner harmony. That assurance combined with assistance of his spirit guides helped him to transition to the next dimension.

Astral Parasites

Just like we have mosquitoes and leeches in the physical world, there are parasitic entities that reside in the middle world that draw power and energy from us. Usually they do that without our knowledge. It would be wrong to assume that they are always malevolent. While there are entities that might wish to steal energy and who do have negative intent, the vast majority of these parasites are more like mosquitoes looking for food. Unfortunately, sometimes our energy may be the food for those entities. This can affect our health and well-being, so we want to prevent them from taking our energy. These astral parasites can only suck energy from us in places where we have holes in our auric field.

A shaman once told me that an arrow or 'negative energy' can only go in where there is a hole. These holes are caused by beliefs created by traumas. When we have traumas happen, often a part of the spirit leaves the body and we have power loss or what some might call soul loss. This loss of power or loss of soul fragments can be likened to an abandoned building. An abandoned building is a more likely target for vandalism and theft because there is no one there to protect it, whereas a house full of people with all the lights on is much less likely to get broken into. When we are full of our power, we gain immunity against negative spiritual influences. When we have power loss or soul loss, it creates a hole in the energetic field that opens a doorway for spirit intrusions to enter or parasites to feed. It also creates a leak in the containment field, which in turn, creates greater losses of power. This power loss can cause physical, emotional or mental illness. Shamanic healing helps the person to regain power and the protection that power provides.

Soul Retrieval

In a middle world journey, a healer can extract the negative intrusions, assist the person in calling back the power or soul fragment, and seal the energetic field. In shamanic lingo, this is often referred to as *soul retrieval*. When a soul fragment leaves the energetic body, it often migrates to the lower world, the upper world or occasionally another location in the middle world as a way of removing itself from the potential of recurrence of the trauma within a particular incarnation. In a shamanic journey, the shaman will travel to find that soul fragment. It often appears as a version the self at the age it was when the original trauma occurred. The shaman must then provide healing and reassurance to that soul part so that it feels safe enough to return to the middle world and to the body energetic. After the shaman has encountered and interacted with the soul part, s/he will lead this soul fragment back to the middle world and to the body energetic and then integrate it with the person receiving the healing on either or both subconscious and conscious levels.

The Practice of Divination

Another action that is performed in the middle world is divination. Divination is the ability to see not only what is but also the potential reality of what can be. Any psychic act that sends us through the timeline for information can be considered a form of divination. Considering that we are in the free will zone, there is very little about the future that is cast in stone. But based on choices of the past and tendencies of mind, there are certain realities that are more probable than others.

Future divination is a charting of the most probable reality based on the tendencies and beliefs of the past and present. Most divination, however, is a fine grasp of what is currently occurring. With good divination, a person may acquire a broader perspective of a current situation in order to make good decisions. Divination can give us insight into our "blind spots," helping us to see what our conscious mind is rejecting. With this information in hand, the individual is more likely to make good choices to bring about the desired result in the future.

The Merit of Shamanic Practice

Through journeying to the three worlds of non-ordinary reality, we can experience the multidimensionality of our existence. This awareness gives us the broader perspective necessary to transform our emotional, spiritual, and mental state, and thereby transform gross physical reality.

We begin as light and energy, and we ultimately return to that state when we recognize the true reality of our union with the Divine. Expanding our awareness beyond third-dimensional linear reality increases our awareness of nonphysical reality. By doing so, we can experience more of our larger nature beyond the third-dimensional construct.

4

Balancing the Intellect, Passion, Emotion, and Body through the Elemental Forces of Nature

Fire, water, earth and air are the basic elements from which all creation is made. Plants need sun, rain, earth and air to nurture and sustain their life and growth. Humans and other animals could not survive without the warmth of the sun, without the abundance of food from the earth, without water to drink, nor could we live without air for more than several minutes. These are the basics upon which we depend. We are composed of the elements, and they give us a strong foundation on which to build our lives. The number four symbolizes strength and stability, and the four elements represent the strength and stability of a well-planned structure.

These four elements represent different aspects of our being: air, the mind, fire, the spirit, water, the emotions, and earth, the body. When we attain a balance of all these aspects of our lives, we are able to achieve greater balance within ourselves, with the people around us, with our life situations, and with the Earth.

Each of us is influenced by our relationship to the elements. Usually, some of the elements influence each of us more than others. For example, some people are very fiery and throw themselves fully into what they are doing, but in the process, "burn out" from overextending. Another person may have a very intellectual or air-oriented approach to life but have a hard time getting in touch with their emotions. One way to approach our personal growth is through balancing different aspects of our persona by balancing our relationship to the elemental energies.

Many people are imbalanced elementally in some way. Some have an excess of a particular elemental energy, and some are lacking in a particular elemental energy. It is possible to learn how to achieve balance between the four elemental energies by moderating their various excesses and enhancing the qualities we lack. It can be achieved both by working with the related elemental force through elemental meditation and by the balancing of activities and proclivities that relate to the elemental natures.

Elemental Influence Quiz

Here are some questions to help you clarify your elemental strengths and weaknesses. Respond to these questions on a scale from one to five, one being not very true for you, five being very true for you. Go with your first impression if you are not sure. First impressions are often the most accurate.

1. I cry easily.
2. I find it easy to tap into my creative energies.
3. I have strong will power.
4. I like to daydream
5. I find it easy to communicate my thoughts.
6. I find it easy to express my feelings.
7. I take good care of my possessions.
8. I feel that I am in touch with my body and its needs.
9. I consider myself to be an innovative person.
10. I am grounded in the here and now; I am not "spacy."
11. I can be very moody.
12. I am passionate about my life.
13. I have a lot of patience.

14. I tend to respond quickly to things I feel I must change.
15. I love intensity.
16. I have a quick mind.
17. It is easy for me to be aware of what others are feeling.
18. I am affectionate.
19. Financial security is a high priority for me.
20. I tend to be very enthusiastic.
21. I work quickly and efficiently.
22. I am very practical.
23. I love spontaneity.
24. I love intellectual challenges.

On a separate sheet of paper, make four columns, one each for air, fire, water, and earth.

Below you will find a key that will tell you which column you should enter the score for each question. You can tally each column to see which of the elements you are most aligned with and which are the most foreign to you.

For each question, you now have a score between 1 and 5. If you marked "4" for question number 1, you would put 4 points in the water column, because question number 1 relates to the element of water.

Here is the key: 1-water, 2-fire, 3-fire, 4-water, 5-air, 6-water, 7-earth, 8-earth, 9-air, 10-earth, 11-water, 12-fire, 13-earth, 14-fire, 15-fire, 16- air, 17-water, 18-water, 19-earth, 20-fire, 21-air, 22-earth, 23-air, 24-air.

Astrological influences can help us see our elemental influences, since the different signs in our charts are ruled by the different elemental energies. If your astrological sun sign is Aries, Leo, or Sagittarius, add two points to your fire total. If your astrological sun sign is Taurus, Virgo, or Capricorn, add two points to your earth total. If your astrological sun sign is Gemini, Libra, or Aquarius, add two points to your air total. If your astrological sun sign is Cancer, Scorpio, or Pisces, add two points to your water total.

Look at the numbers you came up with for the different elements. Did one score turn up particularly strong for you? Did one turn out to be weaker? Are they nearly balanced? Do you see yourself particularly intellectually, emotionally, or materially biased in your outlook in life? Do you approach life with a fiery passion? The answers to these questions should help you to see where you stand on the elemental wheel.

Let's now go into more detail with the attributes and symbology of the elements, as well as some of the metaphors that symbolize the elemental energies.

Air

Air is symbolic of the powers of the mind. It represents knowledge that is gained by both intuitive and intellectual means. Air can bring us wisdom. Its inherent virtues are truth and clarity. Some skills that air brings to us are communication, inventiveness, and the power of discernment. Air also represents speed. Our main access point to air is through breath. The physical sense associated with air is smell.

The natural symbols of air energy are air itself, wind, breath, sky, windy plains, mountain tops, dawn, spring, and the bird spirits, particularly the eagle and the hawk. In the western occult tradition the air spirits are called *sylphs*. The magical tools and symbols of air energy are the sword, the censer, feathers, and the burning of sage and other herbs, resins, or incense.

Misaligned or overemphasized air energy can manifest as overly analytical thought processes, ceaseless mind chatter, and the loss of awareness of emotional feelings due to an overemphasis on thinking, rushing around, and spaciness.

Fire

Fire is symbolic of spirit, or pure energy. It represents transformation in action. It is the spark of our creativity and our passion for life. Fire is representative of the will. Fire's virtues are valor, courage, passion and devotion. Some skills and attributes that fire imbues are purification, will power, the ability to burn away what is not needed, and the ability to heal with energy. Our main access point to fire is through our nervous system and the blood in our veins. The physical sense associated with fire is sight.

The natural symbols of fire energy are fire itself, the sun, flames, heat, electricity, lightening, volcanoes, desert, noon, summer, lions and fire-breathing dragons. In the western occult tradition the fire spirits are called *salamanders*. Some mystical symbols for fire energy are wands, candles and lanterns.

Misaligned or imbalanced fire energy can mean violent outbursts untempered by forethought or compassion for others. People with excessive fire energy often overextend beyond their limits at the expense of other parts of their being or the people around them.

Water

Water is symbolic of the emotions. Love, with both its joy and sorrow, is represented by water. Like water, emotions are sometimes smooth and sometimes turbulent, but always changing. Compassion is one of the key attributes of water.

One of the greatest gifts water gives us is the ability to let in unconditional love so that we may truly learn to feel safe and to trust. In this deep state of trust, we can get in touch with our innocence. Innocence is usually thought of as naiveté, though in this case, we must distill the meaning of innocence down to its roots — in-essence-ness — and the origin of our true self.

Water energy is also symbolic of our own watery depths, the unconscious mind and the powers of intuition. Water reminds us to "go with the flow," moving with what is going on instead of trying to paddle upstream. The physical sense associated with water is taste. The natural symbols for water energy are water itself, oceans, rivers, streams, lakes, ponds, rain, springs and wells, the moon, twilight, autumn, and all creatures that live in and near water. In the western occult tradition the water spirits are called *undines*. Some mystical symbols for water energy are the chalice, cup, bowl, and shell.

Misaligned or imbalanced water energy can manifest as wallowing in emotionality and self-pity, and can create obsession with relationships and romance.

Earth

Earth energy is symbolized by the physical body. As the Earth circles the Sun, the seasons of the year change from new life in spring, to growth in summer, to decline in fall and finally to death in winter. The earth energy represents these cycles in our lives, in our physical birth and death, as well as our little births and deaths that make up the changes of our lives. One of the gifts of earth energy is the ability to be grounded in the now in the midst of change. Earth energy also helps us to live well on the planet. Issues of abundance, sustenance, thrift, acquisition, and conservation are all aspects and qualities that fall under earth's domain. The physical sense associated with earth is touch.

The natural symbols of earth energy are earth (soil) itself, silence, caves, mountains, groves, fields, rocks, crystals, gems, metals, midnight, winter, cows, bulls, buffalo and stag. In the western occult tradition the earth spirits are called *gnomes*. Some mystical symbols for earth energy are the pentacle, disks, plates, and coins.

Misaligned or imbalanced earth energy can manifest as greed, miserliness, a perpetual sense of lack, difficulty with change, and difficulty being on the planet and in a body.

Elemental Meditations

Some of the spiritual systems that work with the four elemental energies assign the different elementals to different directions and represent them with different colors and symbols. Metaphysically speaking, this makes it easier to conceptualize and hold the energies of the elements more concretely in one's mind to work with the power they represent. By placing the elements in a direct relationship to the four cardinal points, it can make it easier for a person to feel, envision and create a circle of power to work with them. Placing the elements in a pattern helps the mind to concretize the process by having a directional anchor.

To work with the elemental energies, it is important to establish a personal connection with each of them. It is not enough to have an intellectual knowledge of their qualities and attributes. To really be able to work with the elements in a more profound way, it is important to connect with them on emotional, physical, and spiritual levels. One of the best ways to do this is to go out in the natural environment and do meditations on the different elements. Here are some examples of some in-depth elemental mediations.

Fire Meditation

The fire meditation is best done with a group but may be done individually if your wood supply is well stocked in advance. Choose a clear or rainless night to do this meditation. Try to do it in a place you will not be disturbed or intruded upon by other people. Prepare a good space to have a fire. Make sure that trees are well out of the way, that you have a good ring of stones around where the fire is to be, and that you have water on hand in case of an emergency. If you have a wand or some other fire symbol, bring it with you so that you can empower it with the energy of this ceremony. In the future, this tool will hold greater power for you because it will remind you of this fire initiation.

Before you begin, place a small bundle of sticks beside you to use during the meditation.

Before lighting the fire, ask the fire elementals to come and work with you and to reveal their inner nature to you. Honor the other elementals, the four directions, and call on the assistance of your spirit guides and helpers. Each person should give an offering to the fire before lighting it. That offering might be tobacco, sage, or any burnable thing that has a sacred meaning for you.

If you have several people present, pass around the matches and have each person light the fire from where they are in the circle around the fire. For the rest of the night, stare unswervingly into the fire. You may sit or stand quietly, dance, drum, breathe or sing with the fire. If you do a more active fire meditation, it is important that your dancing, drumming, chanting or sounding stays focused on the fire and not on the act or interaction of doing those things. Anything you do should be entirely dedicated to fire energy. It is important to stay focused and not get distracted by other things to the best of your ability.

As you gaze into the fire, feel the fire within you. Feel how the fire energy manifests in your life, your personality, and in the world around you. Become aware of your own vitality, your passion for life, and your ability to transform. Take some time to meditate on what you are ready to let go of in your life and resolve to give those patterns, habits, attachments, and concepts to the fire. Hold one of the sticks from your bundle and fill it with what ever you are releasing. When you feel the time is right, throw the stick into the fire to release and transform those stuck parts of yourself. Do this as many times as you need to. When you are done with your fire ceremony, be sure to thank the fire elementals and any other helpers for being there. Douse the fire thoroughly, and leave respectfully.

The more hard core of you may want to do this fire initiation as an all night event. Others may feel more comfortable with only a few hours. Do what feels best. There are a lot of extremes to be had. If you can only get it together to stare at a candle flame for a half an hour, or you want to do this meditation while *fire walking*, be my guest. You are the best judge of the intensity level you need.

Water Meditation

For the water meditation, find a watery place in nature that appeals to you. It can be by the ocean, by a lake or pond, or by a river or stream. Each of these watery bodies has distinctly different energies, so look inside yourself and see what kind of watery energy your soul craves.

For obvious reasons, it is best to do this meditation in the warmer months. Before you start out, be sure to bring with you a good quantity of fresh drinking water, a special cup or bowl, something comfortable to sit on, and a towel and bathing suit if you think you might need them.

Find a place by the water that feels just right, where you will not be disturbed. After settling yourself, ask the spirits of water to work with you and to reveal themselves to you. Give an offering to the water elementals of some flowers or maybe even some of your own hair. Be sure to also honor the other elements, and ask your guides and spirit helpers to be present.

Have your special cup ready. Fill it with water, and drink. Really feel and taste the water. Feel how it nurtures you. Keep the cup near you and drink from it often during this meditation. When you leave this place your cup will help you to remember this experience.

Gaze into the water you have chosen to sit by and observe its nature. Allow yourself to merge with the energy of water. *Be* water. Observe how it makes you feel. Allow the water to wash away all the crusty layers of personality, pain, and experience that have walled you away from your own inner essence. When you are ready, sit, swim, or float in the water. Let your mind become dreamlike. Surrender to the water's flow. Ask the water to open your intuitive abilities to allow a healing vision to present itself to you.

Stay in this place as long as you need to until you really feel at one with water. You may even want to go from one kind of watery body to another to perceive the difference in energy. As always, do what feels "right" to you.

Earth Meditation

The earth meditation will require a little geological research on your part. You will need to find a dark cave away from the sounds of civilization. You will need a flashlight, some clothing that will keep you warm and dry, and something to sit or lie on. If you are going into a deep cave, you may want to tie a roll of string to a tree or rock outside of the cave and unravel it as you go into the cave so that you will be able to find your way back out in case you get disoriented.

Make yourself comfortable as you sit in the dark and silence of the cave. Ask the earth elementals to work with you and reveal their true inner nature to you. Give them corn meal, corn pollen, or quartz crystal. Honor the other elementals and ask your guides and spirit helpers to be present with you.

Become aware of the energy of the Earth. Feel the magnetic force of the Earth as an embrace that keeps you grounded on the planet. Be aware of your body and its sensations. You may even want to lie down so that your whole body is in contact with the Earth. Open yourself to hear the heartbeat of the Earth. It can take some time before this happens, so be patient.

In the darkness of the cave we can confront our own fears and demons. The overcoming of these fears represents the little deaths that bring us life. The more we can overcome our fears the more we can truly live. The cave is also representative of the womb, gestation, and the promise of rebirth. When we leave the darkness of the cave-womb and move into the light, we are born into our lives anew.

When you are ready to leave the cave, thank the earth spirits and any other helpers you had. Bring with you a rock from the cave to remind you of your experience. If you can't find a good cave, do this meditation deep in the woods during the night.

Air Meditation

For the air meditation find a mountain top, hilltop, or open field to lie in where you will be away from human activity. You will want to bring something to lie on, and sunglasses or other forms of sun protection if you think you will want or need them. Choose a clear day in which you can look up into the limitless blue of the sky.

Ask the air spirits to work with you and reveal their true nature to you. Give them an offering by burning some sacred herb or resin, such as sage or copal. Honor the other elementals and ask your guides and spirit helpers to assist you.

Lie down and look up into the sky. Feel the breezes on your body; be aware of your breath. Breathe in and out, acknowledging the air as it moves in and out of your lungs. Breathe in and out of your heart, getting in touch with the truth you hold there. Allow your breath to awaken the truth you hold in all different parts of yourself. Ask the air elementals to open you to your own spark of perfect wisdom. Listen to the winds for answers to the questions of your life. As you breathe, imagine you are being filled with the wisdom of spirit.

Bring a special feather with you to remind you of the power of the air spirits. In some traditions, a knife, or athame, is used to symbolize the mind's ability to cut through to the truth. If you are of this ilk, you can bring one along to empower with the air energy.

Stay for as long as you feel the need. Be sure to thank the spirits before leaving.

It is good to leave some time between these meditations. I would suggest at least one month. New moons or full moon days or nights are a particularly good time to do them. The water, earth, and air meditations are best done alone for maximum concentration, whereas the fire meditation can be done alone or with others. It is ideal to spend at least a couple of hours for each of the meditations.

These meditations are not essential to understanding these energies, but they will definitely intensify your experience of the elementals. Even if you modify the meditations to simpler forms or less amounts of time, you will find them very helpful.

The Spiritual Principles
of Manifestation

Five is the number of integration through experience. We humans have been given free will to experience and expand ourselves within the constraints of Divine Law. In other words, we can do what ever we want, but not without consequences. One of the lessons of the number 5 is to cultivate our ability to freely expand ourselves while staying in accordance with Dharma, or the natural flow of the universal energy in alignment with Divine Law. In this way we become Logos, which is the Divine as it is manifested in humanity.

The five senses of sight, sound, smell, taste and touch are the ways we perceive and integrate change in our lives. Through these five senses, we take in the information that concretizes our world view for the better or for the worse.

There are five basic stages of life that represent the different kinds of change we experience. These stages are: birth (beginnings); initiation (individuation); consummation (union with others, with path, etc.); repose (reflection, integration); and death (release of patterns, ego, attachments, and the body). These five stages represent a completion cycle within the circle of change. These stages apply not only to the larger cycle of life but also to our own relationship with any cycle of manifestation within our lives.

The five-pointed star is a symbol that represents the capability to manifest our Divine nature through free will and the integration of life's experience. Through focused attention and intention, we are able to create sacred space, which helps us to integrate life's changes, align ourselves with Divine will, and actualize our capability as co-creators of our own reality.

Integration

At the base of the pyramid there are the four corners, which could be likened to the four elementals. The fifth point at the apex of the pyramid represents the fifth element or *quintessence.* It is the point of integration that synergizes the energy of the four corners of the base. This apex co-joins the elemental forces in order to manifest something new as a result of that integration.

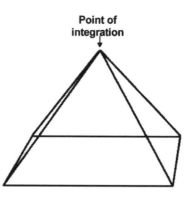

Point of integration

The fifth element holds and controls the elements within itself without being impacted by them. It could be described as a unifying force field. To the Greek philosophers and alchemists, this fifth element was called *ether.* They considered ether to be a binding force that held everything in the universe together, and it was often compared to a cargo ship or boat.[1]

In Hinduism, the fifth element is referred to as *akasha,* which might be thought of as the context or environment which all manifested reality occurs within. Space is the Divine energy filled emptiness that is the canvas for creation. In essence, space is the place. Akasha is considered to be undifferentiated matter containing an infinite amount of energy. It is a subtle state in which energy and matter exist in a dormant state of potentiality. Our reality is governed by time and space. Manifestation is the process of organizing thought and energy through time to make something occur in space.

The Yoga Sutras of Patanjali describe the story of creation in this manner. *Parashakti* (the primordial energy) momentarily separated from Shiva (the absolute awareness) in order to give rise to individuated consciousness. In this separation, *nada* (vibration) *bindu,* (the focal point or nucleus) and *kaala,* (the ray or force that emanates from the nucleus), were all created. This was the beginning of manifest reality through the creation of particle and wave forms. Akasha was created, and then one element then transformed itself into the next. Akasha gave rise to air. Air became fire. Fire became water, and finally water became earth, creating the densest of forms in the universe. The subtle gave rise to the gross. In process of enlightenment, the elements dissolve one into the other the opposite direction, and the gross transforms into the subtle.[2]

The pyramids of the Ancient Egyptians and the Mayans are perfect analogies for focusing and transforming energy to bring about a higher manifestation both in form and beyond form. The apex of the pyramid represents the most refined vibrations. Farther down the pyramid, denser levels of manifestation are represented. Manifest form starts as pure energy directed by thought and the organizing principle of akasha. Over time, that energy / thought becomes more dense, and takes on the cloak of form. Conversely, as we refine our consciousness and move towards our soul awareness, our thoughts become less materially based and more focused on the embodiment of higher qualities and finer vibrations.

Intention + Attention = Manifestation

There is a fine line between thought and matter. In quantum physics, we learn that there is a direct relationship between perception and manifestation. Niels Bohr believed that the occurrence of phenomena is dependent on the observer. In metaphysical theory, we take that concept one step further by saying "Through the laws of manifestation, it is possible to manifest reality according to will by directing thought."[3]

In order to bring thought into form, we must place an intention. It is also essential to focus attention in order to bring about the manifestation of that intention. Intention is the idea, and attention is the awareness or energy. They are not the same thing. Intention is coming up with a clear and concise idea of what is to be manifested. Attention is the act of holding to the course. By doing this, we maintain enough energy around the intention to bring it to pass.

People place intentions all the time, but they often don't come into manifestation for several reasons. In order to bring an intention to fruition, it must be embraced fully. If a person is at cross-purposes in regards to an intention, it is less likely come into fruition. For example, if a person wishes to have a relationship in their life and places that intention, it is going to be much harder for that person to manifest that intention if there is another part of the self that is afraid of having a relationship because of a fear of loss of freedom. Here we have two different parts of the self wanting two different things. Both are steadily working on the manifestation of their goals. One cancels the other out. In order to bring something into manifestation, an essential ingredient is the ability to get all parts of the self in alignment with the intention. (We'll talk more about how to do that in the next chapter.)

The second ingredient is the power of attention. It is not enough to set an intention like a passing thought, it must be maintained. For example, if you want to plant a garden in order to get fruits and vegetables, you can't just plant the seed and walk away expecting that it will bear fruit. The weeds need to be pulled, the plants must be thinned, fertilizer must be applied, and appropriate water must be given in order to have a bountiful garden. Sometimes by just placing intention, you will get a little bit of gain, but to get optimum gain, the placement of attention is important so that one may achieve the highest manifestation possible.

Magical Intent as a Tool for Manifestation

So how do we go about the process of bringing thought into form? Anyone who wants to create anything is working from some sort of methodology to make that happen whether they are aware of it or not. We do it everyday. In order to create a new business we create business plans (intention). We bring together our resources and apply attention to bring about the desired result. All day long, we perform different formulaic rituals to manifest different goals. For example, we take out the toothbrush, put toothpaste on it, add a little water and brush our teeth for the goal of having healthy clean teeth. It is a ritual that most people follow religiously in order to manifest a goal. Likewise, in spiritual traditions, we apply ritual and ceremony to bring manifestation from the vibrational to the physical through different formulas. For example, people pray to a Divine being to bring about healing or guidance. They do this in order to bring about a higher manifestation on the earthly plane as well as a higher manifestation of consciousness on a spiritual plane. All our days are filled with ritual. If we make those rituals more conscious with a deeper focus to intention and attention, the likelihood of higher manifestation is much greater.

As you can see, the applications for what I am speaking about are extremely broad, so let's narrow it down to the ways we can apply this metaphysical knowledge to methods in which we can use our spiritual focus and awareness to bring about higher a manifestation of our life experience. The application of this knowledge can help to effect positive change in the world thereby enriching our spiritual well-being and our physical, emotional and mental health.

All spiritual traditions of the world use different forms of ceremony and ritual as a way to integrate life's experience through the enactment of myth. Myths are the stories, which help us to understand culture and the human experience. Through myth and archetypal imagery we can see the thread of common experience within the culture we live in and within humanity. When we acknowledge the occasions of change in our lives such as birth, marriage, and death with ceremony, it helps us to experience the Divine as it flows through the changes of our lives. It enriches and gives meaning to transformations.

Our lives are constantly filled with change. Ceremony provides a way to integrate and create wholeness in the midst of transition. It creates points of stability that help us to welcome and honor how we have been changed by our experience. These ceremonies can be as simple as blowing out candles and receiving gifts on a birthday, or as elaborate as ceremonies that involve days, weeks, or years of preparation.

We participate in rituals every day without even realizing that is what we are doing. For some, it is the morning cup of tea or coffee that gives the participant an opportunity to pause and have a few minutes of being in the moment of the experience. It is a point of integration. For another, a bedtime ritual might be kissing a picture of a loved one before going to sleep. These simple rituals almost pass without recognition, though they do serve a purpose as punctuation points within the day that anchor us and help to create a sense of stability.

Many people use the terms ceremony and ritual interchangeably. In order to clarify my terminology, I define ritual as a ceremony that is repeated. It is a ceremony that aids in integration through familiarity. If a ritual is performed without intentionality and focused attention, I would be more inclined to define it as a habit instead of a ritual. Rituals that are spoken or enacted with conviction tend to be more effective. For a ritual to be more effective, the participants need to have their full attention and energy engaged in the event. Within my definition, ceremonies are more event-specific. They are not something that is repeated with some regularity. They change according to the occasion for which they are created, the number or focus of the participants, or the energy of the day they are being created or enacted.

Ceremony as a
Transformative Act

Ceremony is a powerful way to create sacred space as separate from ordinary reality. Ceremony makes a powerful statement to the Universe that shows the seriousness of our intentions and demonstrates that we are willing and ready to focus our attention towards a positive goal by connecting to the Divine and our own inner resources. It also is a way to make an impression on the subconscious self that can help to release internal blockages, as well as make positive changes in our lives.

Within a ceremonial setting, we have the opportunity to have experiential contact with non-ordinary reality. It is far more effective to learn something by experiential means than a purely intellectual approach. Experiential learning helps you to integrate information on a visceral and emotional level as well as a mental level.

I remember hearing Indian Saint, Mata Amritananda Mayi say, "It is not enough to read the medicine bottle, you must take the medicine to get well." Reading or intellectually knowing something is not enough to make it a reality. In ceremonial space, we can go into an experiential mode, which imprints and integrates that which is to be transformed in the deepest levels of the psyche.

In many traditions, mental information about a spiritual reality is considered a blockage to true understanding of spiritual principles because it "locks" the information into your own perceptual framework. True knowledge is fluid in nature. It is not to be pegged and defined. In the Tibetan Buddhist paradigm, initiates usually are not given much information about the energy streams they are being initiated into prior to an initiation. Instead, they receive the transmission energetically from the lama and are then given exercises and meditations to work with the energies. In this way, they learn about the energy stream that they have been initiated into by their own experience.

What Can Ceremony Be Used For?

Some common uses for ceremony are:

1. To connect with the Divine and other spiritual beings
2. To mark initiatory transitions in life that are rites of passage having to do with life phases, spiritual transmissions, and spiritual initiations that create change in social rank
3. To align with the cycles of seasons (sun cycles), changes of moon cycles and other astrological influences
4. To heal
5. For purification and cleansing
6. To create positive change
7. For the removal of negative influence
8. Cord making (wedding ceremonies or group bonding)
9. Cord cutting (moving away from old, outgrown, or unhealthy connections or attachments)
10. Integrating different parts of the self.

Sometimes when people do ceremony, they follow a "recipe" that has been created by someone else. Other times, people just use their creativity and intuition to create a formula in order to create sacred space that will bring about change. When the psyche is given a clear set of actions and symbols that it has been familiarized with in a concrete formula, it knows how to respond. This helps the participants sink into the ceremonial space in a way that will make the experience more effective for them. For example, often when people meditate or do ceremony, they may light a particular kind of incense. As soon as that person smells that incense, his psyche says, "Ah, I know where we are going now," and the subconscious will assist the conscious mind in focusing on the transformation at hand.

After years of participating in and creating numerous ceremonies, I have found an effective formula that seems to be the underpinning of many ceremonies. It is the stripped down version that has the basic form with as little dogmatic content as possible, which can be applied to practically any spiritual system with which you feel aligned.

How to Perform Effective Ceremonies

1. Creation of Sacred Space

If you are inside, clean the room that you intend to do the ceremony in. When you clean the room, it not only changes the quality of the physical space, it also helps to clean up the room energetically which decreases the influence of subtle energies that do not serve the intention that you will be setting. It also clears away distractions from the intention as well.

It is a good idea to unplug the phone and choose a time to do the ceremony when it is less likely that people will be dropping in. Decreasing external distractions helps to increase internal focus. The same goes for working outside. You will want to choose a space that has enough open area for whatever you need to do in a place where you feel free from distraction or interruption.

2. Clearing the Space

After preparing the space physically, you will also want to prepare the space energetically. There are several ways that you can clear the space energetically. You can clear the space by burning incense, herbs or resins. You can use sound such as vocal toning or using chimes or singing bowls. It is also very helpful to take some deep breaths to clear your internal space.

3. Centering

Centering your energy will help you to be more fully present and focused. Centering your energy can be achieved by doing simple meditations such as feeling your connection to the earth. You can imagine that you are growing roots from beneath you down into the earth , then draw the energy of the earth up into your body. This will not only help to center your mind and bring you present in time and space but will also ground your electrical body. I have heard it said that you can only fly as high as you can be grounded. When your electrical system is grounded you can experience and connect with the numinous and then bring that energy into form for full conscious integration and manifestation.

Another technique that is helpful for centering is to imagine that there is a central star of energy within you that you can focus your attention on. Imagine you can feel the center of the center, of the center, of your self. This is especially useful for many people because most people in western society are so focused on external goals.

By focusing on the center of the self, you will be able to bring your energy and awareness completely home. Having more of your energy awareness present in one place, it makes it easier to bring about the manifestation of your intention.

4. Creating the Container

By creating the container we define the sacred space in which we perform the ceremony. By defining the sacred space, we clearly announce to our own psyche and to the Universe that we are demarcating a boundary between the worlds. We are creating a time and space outside of ordinary reality. This will help to keep out external influences and can act as a containment system for the energy and awareness that is being cultivated within the circle. Just like an egg must have a shell to protect the growing chick, this container creates an energetic shell that protects and contains the growing creation of the intention and its descent from energy to matter.

There are many ways that you can create this energetic container. Some people imagine that they are in a bubble of light. Other people use some physical substance sprinkled in a circle to demarcate the edge of the sacred space. Some common things that can be used to mark the space are salt, flour, or corn pollen. Other people might direct a line of energy around the circle with a crystal, a wand, a staff, ceremonial knife (athame), or their finger. Someone else might just walk in a circle as a way of demarcating the space. Often, people like to create the circle moving in a clockwise direction (from left to right). If you are working with a group, simply holding hands and setting the intention of creating the container also works just fine.

5. Welcoming Divine Influence

In this phase of the ceremony, the participants call in different positive influences appropriate to the tradition or the beliefs that they operate within and/or beings from non-ordinary reality that relate to the intention being set. For example, at this point, the participants might call in the elemental energies that we spoke of in Chapter 4, deities, ancestors and other spiritual helpers. In some traditions, people like to provide offerings to these beings. For some that might be beautiful flowers, incense, or food.

When calling in these beings, it is important to not just be going through the motions. Engage your senses and your full awareness as if you are truly consciously connecting with these influences whether you are at a level that you can actually perceive them consciously or not. Remember, *imagination* contains the word *magi* which refers to the *magic*.

6. Stating Intention

Stating of intention in sacred space has great power. Whatever you say or think inside of sacred space has import and impact. So be careful what you wish for or think about because it is more likely to come to pass. When you are doing a ceremony, it is important not to have too many intentions going at once, as it will dilute the power. Long before you even began to clear the space for this ceremony, you should have already figured out exactly what your intention is and clarified it. Distill your statement of intention to a direct and simple phrase. That simplicity has power. By making the intention complicated, it can make the process of manifestation more complicated. Keep in mind that not everything has to be spoken. Things can be done in song, through theatre, or poetry. The intention can be stated with a piece of art, form of movement or dance or other expression. Let your creativity have free reign. I have heard it said that the soul speaks in the poetic language of symbology. Any way that you can express an intention that engages your psyche is likely to be effective.

When you are formulating your intention be mindful of the laws of karma. You can manifest whatever you want but remember that you will be responsible for whatever you create. Don't ask for anything you are not willing to take the consequences for.

7. Raising the Energy

After placing the intention, it is time to focus attention. The focusing of attention helps to raise enough cosmic energy to ultimately bring something to pass. Some ways that you can raise energy are by some focused creative meditation such as drumming, chanting, dancing, breath, visualization, or the creation of art. Whatever way that you raise energy should help to continue to focus your attention on your intention. For example, if your intention was focused on some form of personal healing, perhaps you would do a chant to a deity whose focus is on healing. For the same intention, you might use visualization and breath to cultivate energy within your body that you then can use for physical, emotional or mental healing.

8. Energy Climax

At a certain point, the energy that you are raising will have a moment of climax. You might figuratively think of this as the 'orgasm' of the ceremony. When the energy climaxes, it ripples out into the Universe in a burst of power that will rebound into your life in the form of manifestation. This is not something that you can necessarily time. It is one of those things that you just feel intuitively. It is a sense of ultimate expression or highest energy or completion. When this moment feels like it is growing close, the participants should apply their attention and intention to the fullest of their capability to give that release its full strength.

9. Integration

The integration phase of the ceremony is essential in order to transform the blueprint of the intended manifestation into form. It is the reorganization of beliefs, energy patterns, and the flux of the time-space continuum that moves the intention from pure thought to manifestation. In the integration phase, it is particularly important to place the concept of the intention into the context of present time.

By placing the intention in present time, our energy body and our thoughts can reorganize around the idea in a more sensory and thus experiential mode of perception. For example, if you were working on manifesting a new job, in the integration phase you would imagine and feel as though you were already in the job, experiencing the satisfaction of doing something that you love. You might also feel what it is like to experience an influx of abundance from your livelihood. If your subconscious mind and your conscious mind come together to frame something as a fact, the energy that your body mirrors out into the world reflects the desired manifestation back.

From this point on, whenever you focus on the intention it is best to continue to perceive the desired outcome as a present time event. It will reinforce the beliefs, attitudes and energies of the desired manifestation, making the likelihood of it coming into form much greater. The integration phase can be carried out in many different ways. Use your creativity to expand the ways in which you approach this experience beyond merely a mental exercise. You might paint a picture, dance a dance, write a piece of prose, etc. There are as many ways as there are people.

10. Gratitude

Gratitude and appreciation not only reinforce the integration but they are also a way we can offer energy exchange with the Universe for the gifts that are being given. The Universe provides the essential energy and wisdom that we need, and in return, we give our love and thanks.

Acknowledgment strengthens the bonds between both the seen and the unseen realms. It also furthers our conscious connection to forces larger than our limited ego perception. Gratitude is not only something that we can express to things and beings other than ourselves, it is also important to acknowledge ourselves in the process. There is more than just the conscious ego self involved in this ceremony. There are many aspects of the self that are needed in order to bring something about. When we acknowledge and appreciate the energy and attention of all of our different selves, it empowers those parts to assist in the goals that are set and can positively affect the unification of the self. When you give gratitude, make it as heartfelt as possible. Try to engage yourself emotionally as well as mentally. This has more power than just a rote-spoken acknowledgment.

11. Ground the Energy

In the course of a ceremony, we have generated a lot of energy and extended ourselves beyond our everyday ordinary reality consciousness. Now it is time to bring consciousness fully back into form. In order to transform energy into matter, we practice grounding, which helps to connect the integrated energetic blueprint of the manifestation with the earthly magnetic field.

There are several ways to ground. You can imagine that you draw the energy you have raised in through the top of your head, and then draw it down through your body. Send it down into the earth through your foundation. Some people like to place their hands on the ground or lay down flat on the ground as a way of anchoring to the earth and re-establish connection with ordinary reality. Otherwise, you can also do this while standing.

Different people think of grounding at the end of ceremony in different ways. Some people like to think of it as giving back to the earth the extra energy that you raised that you don't need yourself. Others think of it as moving from the astral to the physical realm. Some think of it as the energy coming into form while others see it as some combination of the three.

12. Releasing and Acknowledging Divine Influence

Whatever we call in, we must acknowledge and release. In ceremonial context, devocation or releasement is another opportunity to acknowledge and appreciate the forces that have assisted in our positive intentions. It is not to say that they cannot come and go of their own free will, but when we make a clear juncture between non-ordinary and ordinary reality, it can help us to maintain the boundaries between the realms, which decreases confusion and clutter between the different aspects of our lives. This is sort of like putting away your cosmic toys after a good play session so that there is a clean slate to start with next time.

13. Dedicating the Merit

Dedicating the merit is another opportunity to practice reciprocity with the Divine and to expand the benefit of the ceremony to others who may need the energy and intention placed as well. When I dedicate the merit, my prayer often goes something like this: "May the energy that we have raised benefit all beings that need it. May all beings know peace. May all beings know love. May all beings receive the healing that they need." Feel free to make up your own offering in the way that seems best to you.

14. Opening the Circle

Just as you took the time to create a circle in the beginning, it is important at the end to also release that demarcation. In the beginning, we talked about this sacred circle or shield to be like the shell of an egg. It is time for that baby bird to be born. In order for the manifestation to be born, it must break out of the shell to come into manifestation. Releasing the circle is a part of the birth process and a continuation of bringing energy into form. It is so wonderful to be within the containment of that circle that some people would just like to leave that circle up and active. It is important to know that you can recreate that safe space anytime you like. If we attempt to stay in a spiritual/astral awareness all the time, it is much more difficult to live in the world and to bring things into form. As the Buddhists say, "Before enlightenment, chop wood, carry water. After enlightenment, chop wood, carry water." It is okay to leave the mountain because the mountain will always be there.

To open the circle, it is a good idea to undo the circle in a similar yet opposite way to the way that you constructed the circle in the first place. You can imagine the boundaries dissolving or some people like to remove the demarcation in a counterclockwise or right-to-left direction. Do whatever feels right to you. The most important thing is to visualize and direct the energy of opening the circle and not so much the means by which you do it

After doing ceremony, it is often a good idea to have a little something to eat and drink as a way to continue the process of grounding and re-entering ordinary reality with your consciousness.

You may want to help to reaffirm your intention in the days after the ceremony by placing your attention on something that was in the ceremony. You can do this by placing the artwork you might have created on the wall, feel and visualize your intention as if it is already manifest in the now, or repeat an affirmation that was contained in the ceremony as a way of reinforcing your intention.

The Gifts of Sacred Space

There are many benefits to be gained from ceremony beyond the manifestation of a particular intention. In ceremonial space, we step into awareness of non-ordinary reality in a way that our day-to-day consciousness does not allow. It makes a powerful statement to our psyche that says,  "This is special. This is sacred." When we can impress the subconscious, we can access the power held in the deep recesses of our psyche.

The shamanic traditions of the Yaqui and Toltec people of Mexico talk about the *nagual* and *tonal* realms. The *tonal* is our logical, ordinary reality and the *nagual* is the non-ordinary realm of energetic awareness. In ceremonial space, we step from the tonal into the nagual. When we are in a nagual context, it is much easier to learn about subtler levels of energy and the essences of being than in ordinary reality. It heightens our awareness of these fine vibrations that in the tonal we would not even notice. The unseen becomes more tangible. This context provides access to other ways of thinking and experiencing reality that expands our consciousness to multidimensional awareness. This ceremonial space tends to inspire the participants towards a more spiritually developed state of being and creates internal matrix changes that can reach beyond the energetic and into the tonal frame of reference. Within this subtle awareness, a gateway is opened to our consciousness revealing other realms and the beings that inhabit them.

When we do ceremony with other people, it increases the possibility for change exponentially. It rarifies and intensifies the available energy. If you have only one person, you have that person's energy plus whatever power that person able to cultivate at his or her current level of evolution. If you have two people, the energy is not only doubled, it is multiplied by itself. There is greater power available in the form of the collective . When we join together with a group, that energy has more power to create change through the morphic field, ultimately making change for our entire species.

When we join together in a common intention, it weaves us together not only with a common goal but creates an energetic container that can support us even when the group is not gathered. When a group comes together, it creates a unity of souls that manifests an over-lighting spirit of consciousness that is the sum of all its parts. The more a group meets, the stronger this over-lighting spirit grows, and its ability to create change also grows stronger. In a habitual meeting of souls, the psyche will often find it easier to drop into nagual consciousness out of familiarity . The psyche recognizes that context which strengthens its ability to connect to the over-lighting spirit of the group, also known as the wraith energy. For this connection to be the most effective, it is very helpful to interact with the group in the most mindful way possible so that subterranean emotional material does not get in the way of spiritual working.

Like a family, groups will always have their internal struggles that are often based in the needs of the subconscious to work out internal dynamics externally. With this in mind, it is often a good idea for people to do their best to put away personal motivation and put foremost what will serve the collective. It is good to keep the energy as clean as possible. Being in a group is a great exercise in recognizing that our environment is a mirror for our own psyche: both our most enlightened and beautiful parts and our most shadowed aspects.

When creating ceremony, it is important to be aware of what is essential versus what is stylistic. Don't get lost in the details. When I am creating a ceremony, I think of the format as more of a framework or a guide than an imperative. When we get attached how things are "supposed to be," we lose track of our real intentions and the flow. An important part of being a good ceremonial leader is the ability to be flexible and to track the choreography of energy instead of always trying to order and control it. Applying the tendencies of the tonal realm of logic, order and control do not always fly so well when we step into non-linear reality. The only moment that counts is now. What you wrote and thought before the ceremony is not necessarily the energy you will find yourself in once you arrive in sacred space. It is fine to have a general framework but do keep your sense of humor and a lightness of being even in the face of intensity.

May the manifestation of your dreams bring you joy and align you with your soul's purpose.

6

Merging and Mirroring

The number six relates to the principle of merging. It symbolizes the union of the polarities. If we transpose the six-pointed star into a three-dimensional form, it becomes two interpenetrating pyramids. This *star tetrahedron* is a tantric symbol for the union of opposites. The upward pointing pyramid represents masculine energy, and the downward pointing pyramid represents feminine energy. Tantrics use this geometric form to symbolize the heart chakra, which is the energy center that connects us to everything through the power of love.

Six is a number that connotes relationship: relationship with self, relationship to others, relationship to the world, and ultimately, relationship with the Divine. It represents the perfect balance that creates equilibrium and harmony. The 6 principle heralds harmony both internally and externally. This harmony extends to situations, to people, to plans and to environments. This harmony is most easily found by looking within for the answers. Inner harmony is often a reflection of the balance between our material and spiritual focuses and between opposing desires and inclinations. It is the reconciliation between different aspects of the self, and it is the reconciliation between the self and what we perceive as "other."

When we achieve inner harmony, we naturally experience more harmony in our worldly experience. Our external worldly experience is a mirror of our internal state. This harmony is achieved by the healing that reconciliation brings. Coming to a state of peace and balance requires refinement and adjustment of our perspective and attitude.

If We Have the Power to Change our Lives,
Why is it so Hard to Do?

The answer lies within. Different parts of the self have different motivational factors. The conscious mind has agendas about what it would like to create in our lives as well as fairly clear ideas about what it believes about the nature of reality. Unfortunately, the inner psyche has different agendas about what it wants to create and what it believes. Sometimes, we are somewhat privy to what those unconscious motivations are but have not figured out the keys to transforming those agendas, beliefs and feelings. Other times, we have no clue what the motivations of our psyches are because we have not yet learned how to pay attention to those subtle promptings.

Since your subterranean psyche is participating in dictating what you are manifesting, it would serve you to know what your hidden motivations are. That way, you can begin to align the different parts of yourself with the things that will serve your highest interest. This will help you to transform your reality from an integrated perspective.

Everyone is a Multiple Personality

We have been led to believe that only the mentally ill have multiple personalities, but in fact it is perfectly natural and normal for a person to be operating from many different perspectives. There are different levels of dysfunction. Some people are more and some are less integrated between their different subpersonas.

People get into problems when the different subpersonas are each doing their thing without a centralized observer-self maintaining witness consciousness. It is more likely to be classified as mental illness when the subpersonas are going about their business without the other parts knowing what they are doing.

Most people know they have split motivations but have not yet acquired the skill to modify the choices those internal parts are making. In order to become more integrated, it is important to look within and begin to understand some of the ways that we split internally in order to cope with all that life brings us.

Each of those personas is acting out an agenda. Often, these agendas are at odds with one another. For instance, let's say that there is a person who would love to become a famous rock and roll star, but one of their subpersonas is terrified of being rejected so it has developed a habit of trying to hide in order to stay safe. That person is going to have a pretty hard time being publicly visible if the inner agenda is to be invisible in order to stay safe. Here we have a clear schism, making it more difficult for that person to manifest a conscious goal.

In Chapter 3, we began the process of understanding different levels of inner division, the sum of the parts making the whole. Let's now divide the subconscious up into several likely subpersona structures that tend to affect the average person.

The Child Self

The first and most important subpersona is the child self. The child self is involved with the most primal sense of self-preservation. The dysfunctional emotional states it is most likely to be feeling are sadness or fear. Fear is usually the first reaction to a trauma that we have. That first reaction is the initial response that keeps us in bondage to a pattern. Often such patterns are recreated in a loop and we experience them again and again. Some people never cut free of that initial response. Others, after applying much attention and intention are able to transform those primal responses through emotional and mental healing processes or by the practice of compassionate witness consciousness. The child self often needs love, support and understanding as a means to transform its negative state.

The Rebellious Teenager

The secondary subpersona is a part of the self that is in reaction to the initial response of the child. This persona creates a response pattern as a way to cope with the initial trauma. In psychological lingo, this is called a "reaction formation." This persona can be likened to the teenage self, though its patterns do not always originate from that time period in a person's life. This name refers more to the way a teenager might react. It is an act of rebellion that helps to create change, which is sometimes for the better and sometimes for worse. A good

example of this teen reaction formation might be of a boy who felt ostracized and scared of his peers as a younger child. Later on, he became a smart-aleck tough guy to compensate for feeling small, powerless and inadequate. In one way, this reaction has served him because he is now much harder to take advantage of. The negative aspect is that he may have developed knee-jerk response pattern to interactions with others. There are many times this reaction may not be at all appropriate or helpful in his overall life. Similar to most real teenagers, this teen self almost always believes it is right and tends to be a bit stubborn. In order to transform its righteous need to react, it requires a little extra convincing and cajoling.

The Inner Judge

A third subpersona is the inner judge. The inner judge is the one who slaps us around to try to get us to straighten out our ways, to "get with the program." This part of the persona always "knows better" and is invested in disciplining different parts of the self which, by its assessment, might cause lack of love  or lack of success by going against the agenda. This is a subpersona that many of us are all too familiar with. Even though we may be aware we are beating ourselves up over something, most people still don't have control over it anyway. The judge just keeps hammering away no matter what we think or feel to the contrary.

The Fixer

Another subpersona is what we might call the "adult rationalizing" pattern, or the fixer. This subpersona spends many long hours trying to rationalize and problem solve, trying to figure out how to strategize a way through any problem. This over thinking is a good way to drive yourself crazy. Scenes and possible interactions are run over and over in the head in order to figure out appropriate action.

Meditations for Contacting the Subpersonae

These subpersonae are parts of the psyche that can be visited, conversed with and transformed through interactive creative consciousness processes. This work is essential for integrating and aligning these aspects with your conscious intent.

Healing Meditation for the Inner Child

Take a few deep breaths and bring your awareness to the sensations of your body. Notice how you feel, from the top of your head to the bottoms of your feet. All emotions have sensations that accompany them. Notice how you feel emotionally. Just completely relax and sink your consciousness deeper and deeper into your body-mind awareness. Place your hands in the center of your chest, at the location of your heart chakra. Adopt an attitude of compassionate loving kindness towards yourself. Feel the love that you have for yourself. Focus not only on the *idea* of loving kindness, but also on *feeling* the sensation of loving kindness that you have for yourself.

Take a moment to review your life and note any repeating patterns that have manifested. This pattern may be how you interacted with a particular person or people. It may be situations that have occurred repeatedly or how you repeatedly reacted in certain situations. Choose one of those repeating patterns to focus on. These repeating patterns are like beads on a necklace, events that are strung together by a thread of similarity. Travel back through each of these events and try to remember the first time that you felt this way or a similar event occurred. Put yourself back in that scene and remember how it feels to be you in that scene. Notice the sensations in your body. The sensations in your body will help you to connect with how you felt emotionally. Notice which emotions you feel when you reconnect with this moment in time. In this meditation, you will be able to connect with the memories, sensations and emotions enough to stimulate your awareness about the event without really re-living it. It will be as though you are watching it from a comfortable distance, close enough to be aware of what is going on but far enough away so that you feel completely at ease and relaxed even though at that time it may have been painful or frightening.

Does this sensation-emotion have a location in your body? Place your hands on that location if you are aware of it. Sink your awareness deeper into this sensation and/or location. Imagine a younger version of yourself is living in this part of your body. You may see this child, feel this child, hear this child, or some combination of the three. Don't worry about getting this right; whatever you experience is fine and exactly what it needs to be.

How old do you think this child is?

What physical position is the child in?

How do you feel when you see this child?

What does the child need in order to feel complete, whole and healed? It may be something that you can offer to the child right now or something that you might do in your everyday life that will help this self feel more complete.

Can you give the child what it needs?

Notice how you feel towards the child. Do you want to love it or make distance from it? See if you can contact that loving kindness that we focused on before and give that same loving kindness to the child. Imagine that your heart is pressed up against the heart of this child and imagine that the energy of loving kindness is radiating from your heart into the child's heart. Feel and see the energy of the child transforming with this loving kindness. If the child had any other requests that you could fulfill right now, imagine yourself doing those activities with the child now.

Imagine what the child would be like if it was completely healed and whole. Come up with an affirmation for the child that describes this fully healed state. It might be something like "I feel completely loved" or "I am safe in my world". Now imagine that both you and the child not only say these words but also feel them as if they are the absolute truth right here and now.

Give the child one last hug for now and know that you can return to this place whenever you want. Allow your awareness to come all the way back into your body and back to the place where you are doing this meditation. Take your time to return completely noticing sounds, sights, smells around you.

Imagine how different your life will be once this child self feels completely whole and healed. I have heard it said that this child self is actually your High Self. When the child is healed, you reach enlightenment. Take a nice deep breath and ground yourself in ordinary reality, knowing that you have brought a powerful key for healing and integration back with you.

To continue this healing process, it is important to make a commitment to follow through on fulfilling the child's needs for safety, love, security, etc. in your everyday life. Can you make a commitment to follow through with nurturing activities that will help this part of yourself to grow and heal? Checking in with the child self regularly and giving love and attention is one activity that is likely to help heal your child self in a significant way.

Re-Decisioning Process for the Teen Self

Your teen self responds to traumas with a coping pattern that helps you to manage your emotional state and gives you an action-related way to feel as though you are in control of the situation. Consider some pattern that started in your childhood. Perhaps when you were an adolescent or teenager, you came up with a way to deal with that problem. Perhaps you became distant or aloof or maybe you got angry. Maybe you learned how to placate people, or maybe you learned how to bend the truth in order to get what you wanted. What pattern do you think might have created that could help you to feel like you are in control?

What way did you respond to what life was dishing out? When this life situation came up, what conclusion do you think you might have come to about how life works? For example, "Life isn't fair." "People are mean." "Nobody listens to me." "I have to be sneaky to get what I want."

Imagine that somewhere within you is this teenage self. What does it feel like to be that self? What are the sensations and emotions of the teen self within you? Observe your teenage self from the perspective of loving kindness. From this perspective, what action would serve your greater good better than the one your teenager chose?

Thank this teenage self for trying to protect you. It has always had your best interest in mind even though it might not have had the ideal strategy to deal with it. Observe what would be easier and a healthier way to respond to life's challenges. Ask the teenage self if it would be willing to help you by trying out this new strategy. You may have to negotiate with him or her a bit about this. Try to figure out a solution in which everyone gets what they need. After all, every part of you deserves to happy and feel safe. Teens usually respond best to clear and respectful communication.

Imagine this teenage you responding very favorably to this easier, healthier alternative. Imagine this self maturing, aging and opening to new ideas. This maturation helps this part of you respond to life's experiences in more effective and healing ways. Thank this self for doing its very best to help and protect you.

Quieting the Inner Judge Meditation

It is not at all difficult to access the inner judge. We need only to observe when we are berating ourselves for one thing or another to experience the inner judge. One of the most powerful practices that I have applied to my life is the practice of mindfulness. I do this by being aware of what my mind is saying to me at any given time.

Is there a stock phrase that your inner Judge always says, like "You are stupid," "You are fat," or "You never say the right thing"? These are the kinds of statements that we are watching for. To transform the inner judge, notice whenever the inner judge is saying this sort of thing to you.

At the moment you recognize the inner judge is activated, stop what's happening in your mind, quiet the judge, and practice the loving kindness meditation. You can say something to that part of you that is being berated, which is the antidote or the opposite of the inner judge's statement.

Say something that engages your psyche in a believable way. Maybe you say something as simple as "I love you, it's okay." My stock phrase that I say to myself as an antidote to the inner judge is "You are good." Have it be something reassuring and loving that helps you to feel more at ease within yourself. You will probably have to say it a number of times to get to the point where you can really integrate it.

It is extremely important to not just say the words but to feel the words as a living reality. Repeat the statement in your mind until you can feel a sensation as if your body believes it. One way you will know you have reached that state is that you will feel a sense of release or ease. You may even notice your body has the inclination to take a nice deep breath and let out a sigh of relief. Once you achieve the ability to transform your consciousness and body energy to a state of self love, you will naturally feel more confident and at ease in your life.

I suppose that you could just recognize that you are judging yourself and then stop there, but it is important to realize that it is not just your conscious mind that takes the hit from the inner judge. The child self is the one who mainly takes the hit from the inner judge. It is important to repair the damage as well as stop the negative self-judging behavior.

Fixing the Fixer

Such a large emphasis has been placed on the mind as tool for success in Western society. While much greatness has been achieved through the prowess of the mind, its overrated. Some things can be figured out, but the vast majority of our problems can not be strategized away. Over mentalizing is symptomatic of the psyche attempting to escape feelings by zipping up to the head. Here are some simple strategies to calm the monkey mind:

• Take one day at a time. Don't have your pain in advance by worrying about the future.

• Trust yourself in the moment, instead of premeditating every conversation or move. You might surprise yourself at how well you can do by being spontaneous.

• When you notice that you are overthinking, take a deep breath, and re-center your awareness in your body.

• Take a break. Take time to smell the roses, enjoy the flowers, and appreciate your life. Remember, we're not here to get it right, just to learn, to love, and to be.

External Structures and their Influence on Perception

Our ability to manifest our reality in beauty is not only affected by the different agendas of the subpersonas. It is also affected by external structures in our lives. External structures are the belief constructs held by family or culture that influence our world view and thus influence our ability to manifest reality. Close to the matter are the belief patterns that are generated by our families of origin.

Familial pattern addictions are ways in which we are unconsciously recreating the beliefs and emotional patterns of our parents, our siblings and even our ancestors. Many Native

American peoples believe that anything we do affects seven generations before and after us. The way that we feel, the things we believe in, and how we act affect our children and our children's children and so forth. It is not only our physiological components that are encoded in our DNA. The encodement extends even to how we perceive reality. Some people say our behavior is based in our nature and some people believe that our behavior is based in how we are nurtured. I believe that it is a bit of both.

Familial Programming

The easiest way to make conscious headway into understanding these unconscious patterns is to observe the beliefs and the emotional patterns of our immediate family. Strong influences are imposed by the psychological makeup of those that surround an individual. It begins in the womb. In the womb, we directly experience of all the mother's thoughts and emotions. I can imagine that a child in the womb would often find it difficult to discern its own feelings from its mother's. The birth mother's patterns can influence the individual, not only through genetic encodement but also through the experience of being in the womb.

Once the child is born, it is constantly bombarded by the impressions, emotions and beliefs of those who surround it. The child is like a sponge that soaks up every detail and begins to construct an overall impression of reality based on its surroundings and experiences.

Most people have certain emotions that they think are acceptable and others that they think are unacceptable. If a person was raised in a household where no one ever raised their voice or argued, they would soon get the idea that anger was a completely unacceptable emotion to be expressed. On the other hand, a child who was raised in a family that often had intense and violent angry outbursts might externally choose the totally opposite way of being as a reaction formation, yet internally may be full of rage for how they themselves were treated in their family of origin.

There are often very few half-measures in the ways we relate to emotional states. People usually go with the emotional pattern presented by people from their family of origin or opt for the opposite in cases where a particular emotional state is highly prevalent in the family of origin. Generally, either a person follows the blueprint and externalizes it or rebels against the blueprint and internalizes it, repressing the negative emotional state in the "shadow self." Either way, both agendas are present creating an internal schism.

Cultural Influence

Another external structure that profoundly affects us is the social structure to which we are born. Cultural context is extremely influential. Our social structure in the most primal sense is representative of our "tribe". We are tribal animals. In a tribe, we are highly dependant on each other for survival. To go against the tribal will or tribal taboos could mean punishment by, or expulsion from the tribe, which could mean a loss of life or loss of well being. In our current day society, it seems as though it is "every man for himself," but on the deepest primal emotional levels we are completely intertwined with one another. Adults roll their eyes at teenagers' fixation on fitting in by wearing the right brands, or using the lingo of the current teen culture, but the need to fit in is a basic response to tribal culture and the need for acceptance. On a subconscious level, people are often highly motivated by what other people will think of them and will often struggle to keep up with the tribal norms, both in likes and dislikes as a way to fit in. Two of our most basic fear motivators are the fear of loss of love and fear of loss of life. These are often the goads that help to keep us "in line."

Every culture has its taboos, which may not be taboo from the perspective of another outside culture. For instance, sex outside marriage in western culture is the norm, whereas, in the Muslim world any woman caught having sex outside of marriage could be stoned to death. These societal taboos and beliefs directly affect our ability to create our own reality. Sometimes these taboo actions are not a good choice because of a huge social consequence. Sometimes we do not follow through on taboo actions because we have been taught that something is bad or wrong, and we have not been taught to think for ourselves.

How Do We Change?

There are other subpersonas beyond those that have been mentioned here. These four subpersonas that were developed and formed by the externalizing structures mentioned are only the basics. A useful way to visualize the self might be to imagine all the subpersonas in a circle. In the center is the part of the self that we will call "the observer." The observer perceives reality without positionality. We need the observer's perspective in order to properly bring all of the subpersonas to the light of consciousness. In this way they can be integrated and transformed for the better.

Applying Compassionate Awareness for Transformation

Our first and foremost line of defense in the transformation of consciousness is the ability to apply awareness. By observing our emotions, reactions and beliefs in our everyday life, we can begin to see the patterns that motivate us. Even if you are not the kind of person who likes to sit down and meditate or perform some ritualized spiritual practice, applying the mindfulness of *witness-based consciousness* will help you along the path of enlightenment and support the betterment of your life. Better yet, you can do it while you are going about your daily activities.

To apply mindfulness effectively, it is important to put yourself in the place of the observer with discernment while avoiding judgment. When we perceive reality from a place of discernment, we can see what is effective and ineffective, and that will help us to make better choices in our lives. When we observe from the place of the judge, we tend to condemn or belittle in order to get ourselves into line, which usually gets us nowhere. Observing the self with loving kindness and perhaps a touch of humor is a highly effective way of changing our self-limiting beliefs, habits and emotional patterns.

How Thought Creates Reality

There is a basic chain of events dictated by our nature that is the precursor to action and manifestation. First, we have a thought. That thought is almost always based in some sort of belief system established by our life experience or the external structures we have existed within. Then, we have some sort of emotional reaction to that thought. We like it, we don't like it, it makes us scared, angry or sad, etc. Our body then reacts to that emotion with a cascade of chemicals.

That chemical reaction can cause us to move into our primal *fight or flight* response mechanism. From there we either act or we freeze up like deer in the headlights. The freezing can manifest itself as emotional shutdown, numbing out, addictive behaviors, or as avoidance. If we act, it can either be a constructive action or a reaction formation that we developed as a coping mechanism. Our psyche and our body become addicted to this cycle and reproduce the same reactions in order to get the familiar biochemical response, even if it is one that seems completely at odds with our higher interest. We tend to move towards what is familiar instead of moving out of the box into the unknown. Here is an example of this pattern in action.

Let's say a woman believes she is in love with a man after only a few dates. It has been several days since she has heard from him and she thinks, "I wonder if he will call me?" This tags into an old pattern of fear of rejection that she had in her past. She suddenly begins to feel really sad. A deep, mopey moodiness overtakes her. She thinks, "He will probably never call me again!" and feels a deep sense of hopelessness. Her body is flooded with that familiar biochemical reaction to sadness and hopelessness. She can't take it anymore and so she goes and eats a chocolate cake and falls asleep in a sugar-induced coma of forgetfulness. And so the saga repeats again and again until she is a bitter old woman who has lost her belief that she is lovable and has lost her ability to manifest the love of her life because she is addicted to believing that it is all a lost cause. We all do this to some extent.

Picking the Familiar Poison

It seems so strange that we would choose the same circumstances and emotions again and again, even when they make us completely miserable. It is funny how often we think we are choosing something new, but it turns out that it is the same story with a slightly different twist on it. It is almost as though we have a radar for misery. Really, what we have is a radar for the familiar. Even though we may not like our familiar patterns all that much, at least we recognize them and there is safety in what is known. Moving away from the familiar into the vast unknown is often more frightening than choosing the same old poison again and again. Our unconscious mind chooses these repeating patterns over and over again in an attempt to complete the karma, perhaps to replay it until we get so sick of it that we have no choice but to learn the lesson and move on. A very helpful way to bring these unconscious motivations to the light of consciousness is to directly engage the subpersonas through memory and imagination.

Emotion and Projection

Emotions are a question of choice. We choose to be angry or to fear. No one can *make* us feel a particular way. Placing the responsibility for what we are feeling on things outside of our selves is called *externalizing*. In this situation, we create ourselves as victims and are subject to our environment. If we acknowledge that *we* are the ones who decide to feel anger or fear, we can choose to change our response to external stimuli, and thus we can act in *response* to, instead of in *reaction* to our environment. It is vitally important for us to be aware of our thoughts, emotions, and actions in every moment and to be ever vigilant in our pursuit of consciousness. Any emotion we feel towards others is actually a mirror of how we feel about ourselves. To go within helps us to better understand and heal ourselves within the context of our environment. Applying witness consciousness without any blame and *observing* our emotions instead of *being* our emotions allows us to be the masters of our own destiny.

That Pesky Mind

"The mind is its own place and can make a
Hell out of Heaven or a Heaven out of Hell."[1]
–Milton

Our beliefs are like boxes. Sometimes those boxes can help us to organize the way that we perceive things, creating more ease in our psyche. Sometimes those boxes limit us profoundly. Those energized thought patterns are like holographic prisons that exist within and around the body energetic. Rigid negative beliefs about the nature of reality are the root causes of disease. Repressed feelings and negative emotional states create blockages in the energetic system, which are often the root cause of illness.

It is possible to transform our health on every level by changing the way that we perceive our relationship to reality. For this reason, controlling the mind is essential. Every negative emotion that we feel starts as a thought. If we are able to watch our thoughts from a witness-based perspective, it gives us an opportunity to respond instead of react when emotions arise. We are emotional beings. It is very important to express those emotions and let them pass through us. It is equally important to learn how to express them responsibly in a way that will serve the highest good of all concerned. When we act out of anger or fear, without applying the witness consciousness, we tend to lose our power of discernment.

"We are shaped by our thoughts; we become what we think. When the mind is pure, joy follows like a shadow that never leaves."
— Gautama Buddha

Yes to Now

When we focus our attention on the past or the future, it makes it difficult for us to be fully conscious in the here and now. We lose contact with the current moment. What is happening right now is a microcosm of what has gone before and has the potential for what will be. All the magic is in the present.

Past-oriented guilt and anger as well as future-oriented fear form holes in the energetic body. These holes allow the energy of spirit or *Mana* to flow out, making it harder to manifest things in life. It also leaves places for other energies to enter the energetic field and cause disturbances.

When we live in the present moment, we do not live our resentments and self-hatred over and over again, nor do we have our pain in advance. The present moment offers both the power of perfect redemption and ultimate possibility. In the present moment, we can practice forgiveness because we no longer need to be right as much as we need to be free and to set others free.

Effective Communication

So much of the difficulty between people is directly attributable to an inability to communicate and to listen well. Instead of open hearted communication, people build walls and lash out at one another because they lack the skills that lead to a greater likelihood of getting core needs met. They fall into familiar emotional and behavioral patterns that lock them into repeating patterns within their lives. As a result of feeling insecure, sometimes people create fortresses to keep emotions in and people out.

> "Anger cannot be overcome with anger. If a person shows anger to you and you respond with anger, the result is a disaster. In contrast, if you control anger and show the opposite attitude— compassion, tolerance and patience— then not only do you yourself remain in peace, but the other person's anger will gradually diminish."[3]
> — *The Dalai Lama*

Clear and direct communication is difficult for many people. It means risking vulnerability by expressing feelings and thoughts that the other person may or may not want to hear. It means being willing to hear what the other person feels or thinks without assuming that one person has to be "right" and the other "wrong" if the feelings differ. Two people with different truths can be right simultaneously. Each person's view of reality is that person's truth. Reality is a relative term. When we can acknowledge this, we are well on the path towards cooperation and mutual self-determination. Making conflict productive instead of destructive requires mutual respect for feelings, thoughts and needs. Learning to listen and communicate well allows people to negotiate effectively to get their needs met without manipulation.

If all of life is a mirror of our inner state, we gain power by taking responsibility for what has manifested in our lives. When we take responsibility for our lives, we also take back our power, because we are no longer victims of external situations.

Forgiveness

Many spiritual traditions talk about the importance of forgiveness. Some people get confused and think of repression of anger as forgiveness. Forgiveness is a true release of the anger. Sometimes mindful communication between people can create understanding that paves the way for forgiveness. There are other times when no amount of communication will change the other person's mind or behavior. This is when we must really recognize the true nature of forgiveness. It is important to recognize what forgiveness is, and is not, in order to actualize it. Forgiveness is not condoning. Forgiveness does not necessarily make the other person right. Forgiveness is not forgetting. Forgiveness is recognizing that we do not need our grudges and resentments any longer. Nor do we need our hatred or self-pity. Forgiveness sets us free. Forgiveness is the release of our attachment to the other person being wrong and our attachment to being right.

Every part of the cosmos seeks unity through love and acceptance. Anything we don't accept will simply make trouble for us until we make peace with it.

The Shadow

All of us have a blind spot in our perception of ourselves. Within this blind spot are all the parts of ourselves that we would rather not see. If there are things that you *hate* about other people, they are more than likely hidden aspects of yourself that you hate. You are projecting that out into the world because it is safer to see those things as "other".

We spend a tremendous amount of energy defending ourselves from our own inner darkness. Yet if we were to make forays into our shadow world to clear away the debris of old pain and fear, our shadow self would grow smaller and smaller, thus releasing the energy we used to suppress and contain those parts of ourselves for more creative and constructive projects. Just like a child who fears monsters in the dark, we must turn on the lights to realize our fear is the only monster.

Surprisingly, not only do we have a dark shadow, but we also have a Golden Shadow. These are the characteristics that we project onto others that we admire and characteristics that we believe are beyond our capacity. The Golden Shadow is our own disowned potential. When you experience yourself admiring or being jealous of someone else, it is just an expression of the part of yourself that you would most like to bring into conscious expression in this world. It is within reach. It lives within you. It is like a seed that needs to be nurtured with love and encouragement to bring it into the light of day so you may share its fruit with the entire world.

Life as a Reflection of Perception

All of life is only a reflection of perception. Everything that we perceive is only a small fraction of what is actually occurring.

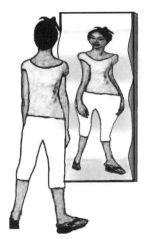

Our perception is limited by our filter, and our filter is limited by our life experience. We are only able to perceive that which is familiar to us. Therefore, anything outside of our world view does not exist for us. That is the reason why two people can be present at the same place and see an event as if it were two totally different events. We can only see what our world view allows us to see. In order to broaden our perspective, it is necessary first to realize that there is more going on than our current perception at hand. That knowledge alone helps to keep the mind open to new possibilities. Taking a step beyond that, it is important to realize that almost everything that you perceive is only a very small fraction of what is the real truth. It is as though we can only see two dimensionally and think that is all there is. We must begin to think multi-dimensionally in order to perceive things from a broader perspective.

Repulsion and Attraction

In order to broaden perspective, we must look deeply at our own prejudices, particularly those that manifest as strong repulsions or attractions. Our attractions and repulsions have a broad influence on the length and breadth of our perception. We are drawn to that which we have attraction towards. Things that we have feelings of repulsion towards, we try to avoid. Anything that we attempt to avoid makes our world smaller. Things that attract us hone our attention in a particular fashion. While there is nothing inherently wrong about having our attention focused in a particular way, it does create limitations.

It is useful to examine what we are trying to avoid. It can help us to get to the root of *why* we are in avoidance. Usually, at the root of these avoidances is a prejudice born either of our experience or of the prejudices of our family or culture. For instance, if you were seen eating with your left hand in India people would think that is incredibly uncouth and disgusting, while in western culture no one would think a thing of it. In some cultures, if a woman's ankles are shown she can be beaten to death, whereas in other cultures, it is perfectly normal for people walk around in the nude. Some prejudices are based in beliefs about health, others are based on religion, and others are based purely on someone's need to decide what is right and what is wrong. When it gets down to it, who's to say what's really right or wrong?

In my life, I have made a point to study many different cultures and religions. It seems that for the most part, each belief system works for its own group even though one belief system may vary widely from another. This leads me to believe that there is nothing inherently right or wrong about any path. What matters more is our perception of reality. Perhaps there is nothing inherently good or bad at all.

In the tantric traditions of India, there is an aspect of tantric practice that some call the *Left-Handed Path* of Tantra. The left-handed path of Tantra believes that all things are ultimately Divine. The left-handed or *Kaula* Tantric practitioner strives to erase repulsions in order to see all things as Divine. It is not unusual for a practitioner of the left-handed path to meditate in a graveyard or engage in other taboo activities. This way, all things become sacred, nothing is outside of the circle of the sacred.

The root of all dualistic perception is the perception of self as separate from the Divine. My personal mythology of the creation story goes a bit like this: In the beginning, the Divine being wanted to perceive itself in the act of creation and destruction. In order to do so, It created the ego mind. The ego's original function was to perceive the Divine. Unfortunately, when the ego mind perspective entered the mind of humanity that split created a lot of problems.

The Ego versus the Divine

The relationship between the ego and the Divine self is very much like the relationship between space and matter. We are actually 99.99% space and only 0.01% matter or form. Similarly, we are 100% the Divine being and the ego mind is the 0.01% of the entire self that perceives us as being separate from the Divine. Stranger yet, the ego thinks that it is 99.09% of the self and it thinks that the self is 0.01% Divine being.

The ego makes decisions about what is "real" based on its perception of phenomenal reality. Those decisions immediately begin to filter out anything that does not fit that view. This severely limits how we perceive reality.

Quantum physics has shown that molecular activity is affected by perception. When physicists would look at the atoms through an electron microscope, they found that the subatomic activity varied depending upon the perceptions of the one who was looking. Our perception alters phenomenal reality.

Metaphysicians commonly believe that phenomenal reality does not exist. It is as though we are dreaming, but we think the dream is actually real. If this is indeed a fact, the ego is creating reality based on an illusion. It is pretty hard to avoid having a perceptual filter in this reality before having achieved complete enlightenment, though it is entirely possible to broaden your perception as a means to broadening your horizons.

It is difficult to not perceive reality from a dualistic standpoint while you are still in a body, just by virtue of the fact that when we place ourselves within time and space there is automatically a duality present. In this dimension, there is a here, a there, a now, and a then. To move outside of dualistic thinking, we must move our consciousness beyond even such basic third-dimensional constructs as linear time and concrete space.

The ego is highly invested in its version of reality and will do anything to protect it. It is more invested in being right about its perception of reality than it is in the well-being of the self as a whole. For instance, if a person was raised with the notion that they are a failure, even though they try hard to succeed, they will self-sabotage and continue to fail because their ego has decided that they are a failure. The body's chemistry, triggered by thought and emotion, reinforces behaviors and biological responses that support the ego's theories about the nature of reality.

The ego always wants to be right, even if being right means being unhappy or sick. Yet, there is hope. Remember, we are 99.99% Divine being and only 0.01% the ego mind. There is a greater truth within us if we can quiet the crazy monkey mind and come to a place of an inner listening.

Re-Centering the Assemblage Point

According to the unified field theory, every unified field (which would include human organisms) has a central location. Some people in shamanic traditions call this place in the human energetic field the *assemblage point*. It is the bio-energetic nexus of our perception. Since we are in a construct of time and space, it can be helpful for us to perceive the assemblage point as having a physical location. The proper location for the assemblage point of soul perception is in the center of the heart chakra. [4] If we focus our attention on the sensations of the heart, we can come into a greater awareness of the perceptions of the heart of the Divine as opposed to our perceptions of the ego mind. The heart is the access point for the merging of all things.

"In order to still the mind, focus on the heart and listen for the listener, who lives in the heart."[5] -Cheyenne Maloney

The heart does not speak in words. The heart speaks in the language of the soul. It speaks in sensation and in symbol. The wisdom of the heart arises not as a thought, but as a sure knowing. The wisdom of the heart brings peace and clarity. It suffuses the psyche with a living experience of the cosmic unity of all things.

Awakening to the Wisdom of Dreams

The energy of the number 7 leads us inwards in order to explore our consciousness with practices such as mindfulness and dream work. Seven represents the growing awareness of our own higher self. Seven represents a solitary pursuit, a separation from the world that is necessary in order for us to understand the mystery of our own psyche. It is the opening of our psychic abilities, awakening new awareness and perspectives. Hence, it is the number of the mystic and the number of wisdom. Part of the way we gain wisdom is through experience and the ability to analyze, assess and evaluate. An ideal way to understand the self is through the vehicle of dreams.

What is the Function of Dreaming?

Since time immemorial, people have believed dreams to be supernatural gifts from the divine, as messages from the spirit world. All religions from both the East and the West have looked to dreams as a source of wisdom and guidance. The Talmud says, "An uninterpreted dream is like an unopened letter from God."

On a psychological level, dreams have been thought of as tools to understanding the deep churnings of the psyche, giving us insight to our deeper motivations, fears, joys, and yearnings. On a scientific level, there are some who believe that dreams are merely the random firing of neurons in the brain that cause the bizarre images of our nighttime wanderings. Others believe that dreams are the brain's way of sorting random bits of information for future use.

There is no easy answer that can explain dreams. I believe that there are many different kinds of dreams serving different functions. Some dreams seem to be a way for the subconscious to process information about life events. Dreams can also be a way for the subconscious to expose the conscious mind to problems it refuses to recognize. After a particularly disturbing dream it is natural for us to ask, "What was that about?" Dreams magnify and intensify feelings and experiences so that the conscious mind will pay attention. Recurring nightmares are a particularly obvious way in which the conscious mind is forced to confront internal demons. The subconscious keeps pummeling the conscious mind with the same or similar images and situations until it gets the point, processing and working out the issues being revealed to us. In dreams, it is possible for us to face the dark mirror of our deepest fears and learn to love the parts of ourselves that seem unlovable.

The dream state is a bridge between the conscious and subconscious minds. Working on dreams helps to build a bridge of communication so a stronger relationship between these two parts of the self may be established.

There are many things we would like to do in life but cannot, due to social mores, personal limitations, or third-dimensional restrictions. Dreams can also be a way in which we can fulfill ideas and fantasies that can produce an inner glow of self-fulfillment even without accomplishing these things during waking consciousness. Dreams can be a release valve for suppressed desires.

Dreams can also be a source for problem solving. Many a person has gone to bed with a question on their mind, waking to find a solution. Sometimes the answer is derived directly from a dream. Other times, we find the answer just seems easier to come by the next day. Perhaps our unremembered dreams held the answer, but the conscious mind got to take the credit for the dreaming self's wisdom!

So much of our experience is focused outwardly on what is going on around us. Dreams give us the opportunity to spend part of each day focused inward. All spiritual traditions acknowledge the importance of dreaming and have spiritual practices that require deep inner reflection. Sleeping and dreaming are nature's way of providing a nurturing inward state. Jung said, "In sleep we return, and through our dreams commune with the rest of creation and the collective consciousness."[1] Dreaming is one way in which we stay in touch with our inner self and our personal sense of connection with all creation. Dream work is a spiritual discipline that follows the inner path. Searching in the outer world for treasure rarely brings true happiness because the true gems of life are found within the self.

Dreams are also a way to commune with spiritual teachers and guides, and sometimes they appear in most unlikely forms. When you learn to look for them in your dreams, their presence becomes more obvious. Often dreams provide spiritual guidance and sometimes they contain prophetic information.

Dream Interpretation

To make the best use of dreams it is important to learn and understand your own symbology system. Dreams are a rich font of symbolic imagery, providing the conscious mind with messages from the unconscious, showing us a language that goes beyond the limits of the spoken word. Symbols are the language of the soul. Taste, smell, sound, color, shape, texture, and feelings are woven together in a tapestry where fantasy and reality blend and merge. Everything is a symbol for something in the dream world, whether it is a literal representation or a figurative metaphor. Dreams often have layers upon layers of meaning. The dream world is a place where the image of a dog can symbolize a quality, a part of the self, someone close to you, a feeling, a life situation, an actual dog, or some combination of these things. These symbols originate from our experience and from the things we have been taught.

Often, we find that we have certain dream symbols in common with other people. Some of these symbols originate from deep within the collective consciousness of humankind. There are other symbols that we share in common with others that are a product of the culture in which we were raised.

Still other symbols are based on personal experience. Perhaps you had a negative experience with a particular kind of dog; your dreams might reflect a sense of danger in your life when that dog appears to you in your dreams later on. Conversely, you may have a positive association with a particular smell. When that smell comes up in your dream, it could indicate a pleasurable experience or association to something else in your dream and in your life.

There are many dream books on the market that have dream symbology dictionaries. While these may help to identify some archetypal symbols from the collective or a particular cultural consciousness, there is no way they can definitively identify what a particular symbol means to you. These types of glossaries are useful tools for generating ideas about the meanings of dream symbols, though it is my belief that the most accurate way to determine symbology is through analysis of your personal associations.

Dream Interpretation Techniques

• A good way to start interpreting a dream is by free association. Think about the symbol; see what feelings or images appear in reaction to it.

You may get several answers. See how these associations can be pieced together with the other symbols in your dream. If a bird shows up in your dream, what images come up to you? Does it represent freedom, independence, flight, fragility, chatter, song, expression, a person you know, or something else? Is the bird caged or free? What does its condition mean to you?

• Review every part of the dream from start to finish as if you are the different objects and people. See what it feels like to be a particular symbol. What do you feel like in relation to the other people, objects and experiences of the dream?

• Think about what happened to you yesterday and what is generally going on in your life. Is there any way in which your dreams might be reflecting your current life experiences or how you feel about those experiences? Dreams are timeless. Past, present, and future can all happen simultaneously in dreams. Sometimes old themes can also appear in dreams that might connect to present issues. See if the theme of a dream seems current or related to some unresolved issue from the past.

• Dialogue with your dream characters. Shut your eyes and imagine that you are having a conversation with one of the characters from your dreams. Ask pertinent questions, like: Are you a part of myself? Do you represent a feeling, a life situation, a life pattern or someone or something in my life? What do you want? How does your situation within the dream make you feel?

Remembering Dreams

One of the first and most important steps in dream work is to be able to remember your dreams. For many people, this in itself is challenging. These are a few techniques that I have found helpful.

Before you go to sleep give yourself a suggestion that you <u>will</u> remember your dreams. Choose some subject you would like to dream about. For example, you might have a question you'd like to have answered or an adventure you'd like to go on in your dreams. Then suggest to yourself that you will have that experience in the dream state. Imagine yourself waking up and remembering your dream. Go to sleep thinking about the dream topic you chose.

Upon awakening, don't move until you have completely reviewed your dream and have all the details straight in your mind. Movement makes dream recall more difficult and represents to your subconscious a call by the conscious mind to move on to the events of the day. Have near your bed some way to record your dream, either a book especially designated as a dream journal or an audio recorder, and document your dream before the memory starts to fade.

Another important way to help remember your dream is to speak it aloud to yourself or to share it with others. When you speak it aloud, you get to hear it as well as see the dream in review, giving you another avenue for remembering. Ideally, it is best to wake up naturally. Alarms can have a jarring affect that can make dream recall difficult.

The Ojibway tribal people sometimes hang a *dream catcher* over their bed to help them to retain the memory and the medicine of their dreams, as well as to help prevent nightmares.[2] Any tool or routine that helps you to remember dreams and improve your dream state is worth using.

These suggestions require some dedication but are well worth the effort. When you pay attention to your dreams, your subconscious will respond to that attention and your dreams will become more vivid and magical, thus giving them the opportunity to relay to you more information straight from the source for your healing and growth. If you regard your dreams as nonsense, your dreams will follow suit and tend to be more nonsensical. The more you honor your dreams as powerful, the more they will tend towards the mystical.

A common pitfall for those who wish to work with their dreams is dream discounting. When we view a particular dream as unimportant or insignificant, we miss the gift we are being given. I have had many occasions when, in my half stupor, I told myself that a particular dream was not important enough to write down, and I promptly forgot it, only to realize later that the shred of a dream I could remember was actually quite profound and significant. At least in the beginning, I suggest you record every dream you can remember, not only for the information it contains, but to exercise your dream muscles. The more dreams you keep track of, the more dreams you will begin to remember every night. You will also find subtle details becoming more refined and easier to remember.

Creative Dreaming

After focusing on remembering and analyzing dreams for a period of time, you may wish to begin taking a more active role in the dream world. Dream work can be a creative process that enlivens both your waking and dream lives. It is, in itself, a spiritual practice.

In today's society, dreaming has not been given its rightful place of power in our lives, so it is more difficult to access the powers available to us in that world. In general, Westerners as a culture have only drawn on dreams for entertainment or psychological revelations. In this rational and linear age, people have become disassociated with the mythic images that dreams provide. Jung said, "If a myth can give life dignity, meaning, and purpose it is serving an important positive function, even if it is not objectively true." [3]

Aboriginal cultures around the world understand the power of myths and regard dream symbols as more than images that reside within the mind. To them, the characters of dreams are real and exist within an actual reality within another dimension. They have ceremonies to induce dreams of power and healing and techniques that honor the power and sacredness of dreaming. Since Westerners do not have the cultural support to remember and work with our dreams, it takes extra perseverance and self-patterning to be interactive with our dream reality.

To be interactive with dream reality, it is important to do things that relate back to the dream while you are awake. Some people act out what happened in their dreams as a way of grounding the dream into waking reality. By doing this they can access another level of memory of the dream through movement and help to integrate the power of the dream through both the physical and mental processes.

Another way to bring the power of the dream to waking consciousness is by making fetishes or replicas of your dream symbols. If you find some particularly strong symbol in your dream, work with it. Find a way to enliven it in your waking experience by drawing, painting, sewing, or making a sculpture of it. This will empower that dream symbol to work with you more in the dreamtime and in your waking life. It will also assist in the revelation of its meaning to you.

Dream State Visualization

Here is a visualization you could do before sleep to utilize the dream state creatively. Imagine you are in a sacred space especially intended for receiving powerful dreams of healing. Become clear on exactly what you are looking for here. Keep your intent focused on one thing that you would like to know or would like to see happen. If you try to create too many things,

your concentration will become scattered, so be specific and ask for one thing. Make a positive affirmation that states exactly what it is you are after, like, "I will receive healing for my sinus condition," or, "My dream will tell me how to heal the sadness in my heart." Become very relaxed and repeat this affirmation to yourself over and over as you prepare to drift off to sleep. Continue to imagine you are in a place that is sacred for dreaming as you do the affirmation. Imagine
that you will be in a sacred place in your dream tonight, and you will receive the guidance and healing you need. Imagine what it feels like to be healed or having received the knowledge you sought in present time.

Lucid Dreaming

It is possible to experience the dream state with your conscious awareness intact. The ability to be awake and aware while dreaming is called lucid dreaming. With lucid dreaming it is possible to change the events and circumstances of the dream. It is also possible to change the way you choose to react to what is going on. As well as being a great deal of fun, lucid dreaming can also be a powerful tool for personal growth and healing. In this state, the dreamer has a supernatural ability to receive information from the inner self, the high self and other spiritual helpers.

In the lucid dream, it is possible to transform negative beliefs about the self that are ingrained in the psyche. The conscious mind is able to reach into the programming held in the subconscious mind and transform patterned behaviors, emotions and concepts. Only when the conscious and subconscious meet are core level changes possible.

Here is an example of this. One woman I know had a reoccurring dream in which she was being chased and could never quite escape. No matter how she would attempt to close and lock doors behind her, her pursuer could push the door open, undo the lock, break the door, or come through the window. Through dream analysis, she concluded that this symbolized her inability to create boundaries in her life with the people around her, and represented the deep fear that she was never quite safe.

Through lucid dreaming techniques, she was able to wake up in the dream and realize she was dreaming. Over time, she became able to lock doors and create safe space for herself. She even had occasions in which she was awake enough to say to her pursuers, "You are only a dream!" and they would promptly disappear. She was even given a magical ceremony in her dream that would protect her whenever she felt unsafe. After a while, she no longer had those disturbing dreams, and she also noticed a change in her ability to deflect other people's psychic, emotional, and physical demands on her in her waking life.

Lucid dreaming is also great for analyzing the meaning of your dream symbols. Once you are awake and aware in your dreams, you can ask the different symbols exactly what they represent to you. Often, if you just ask yourself what something means within the dream, you will automatically know the answer.

It is also possible to merge with the part of the psyche that has all the answers. There have been many famous incidents in which inventions were conceived of, books and stories were created, symphonies composed, and problems solved through dreams. Through lucid dreaming you can actively seek specific information or inspiration towards understanding and creating personal reality.

It has been proven that skills can be honed through visualizing oneself actively engaged in doing what one wishes to accomplish. There are many athletes who spend time doing visualizations of themselves having increased coordination, agility and speed as a means to improving their capacity to excel. Lucid dreaming is an especially vivid way of connecting the mind to the body. Creative visualization within the dream state is helpful with any skill, whether it involves manual, mental, or creative dexterity. In the lucid dream, you not only visualize what you would like to do, it will feel as if you are actually doing it, which is a whole different level of cognition and integration.

You may even choose to lucid dream just for fun. You can go places you've always wanted to go, you can fly through the air, you can meet with a mysterious lover, or you can swim under water with the dolphins. The possibilities are only limited by your imagination. The conscious level benefit of such pursuits is an increased sense of self-assurance. If you know you can create whatever you want in the dream world, that self-assurance can carry over into waking reality. When you know you are the master of your own reality (or illusion, depending on how you look at it), your ability to create becomes magnified.

Lucid dreams have a surreal vividness to them. All senses become magnified, and everything takes on a luminous quality. They are spiritual events. Any dreams with strong spiritual significance I have ever had all share this luminous quality. Lucid dreams are opportunities to experience alternate reality.

The indigenous people of Australia refer to this alternate reality as "the dreamtime." The dreamtime does not refer to ordinary dreaming. It specifically refers to dreams of special spiritual significance that possess a luminous quality, or it can refer to shamanic experiences that occur during waking consciousness. Through lucid dreaming it is possible to access the dreamtime, or non-ordinary reality, while in the deep trance state of sleep.

Lucid dreaming allows the conscious mind the ability to travel in the upper world to meet with teachers, guides, the high self, archetypes, angels, and other enlightened beings for teachings and healing. Often, people find themselves in "school" in their dreams. After awakening in the dream you can call a teacher to you or go to an appointed place in the dreamtime where you will meet with your teachers. To do this, some people walk up a hill, fly upwards, or climb a tree to enter the upper world and meet with these upper world beings.

It is also possible to descend into the lower world to meet with the animal, plant, elemental, and earth spirits for their wisdom. Often in the lower world, the beings and teachings encountered have a profound effect on the subconscious depths of the self.

Sometimes lucid dreaming is thought of as astral travel. Astral travel is the conscious mind, or astral body, traveling through ordinary or non-ordinary reality without the restrictions of the body. In lucid dreaming, we have the ability to travel through non-ordinary reality consciously. It is also possible to wake up enough in the dream to travel through ordinary reality in the astral body. There are healers who travel in their astral bodies to do healing work on others while their bodies lie at home getting some much needed rest.

Lucid Dreaming Techniques

Now that you know some of what is possible with lucid dreams, we will go through some lucid dreaming techniques that can help you to lucid dream.

For many people, lucid dreams will not begin to happen right away, though it is possible that you may do be able to do it on your first try. Lucid dreaming is an art form that requires focused attention and intention. You may give yourself suggestions every night for months before your work begins to bear fruit, so don't give up if it doesn't happen right away.

All of life is a dream. Everything we experience even in our waking life is just an illusion. When we die, we awaken into another level of consciousness about the nature of reality. All spiritual practice is about becoming more awake and aware. The discipline of lucid dreaming is a call to be more awake and aware in both our waking and dream realities.

A beginning point for cultivating lucid dream states is through the recognition that all of life is a dream. This perspective helps to break down the barrier between waking and sleeping consciousness. One way to integrate this concept is to tell yourself as often as you can remember during the day, "I am dreaming." Eventually, this statement will weave its way into the tapestry of your dreams. When you say to yourself, "I am dreaming" while you actually are dreaming, hopefully you will recognize that it is actually true. At this point, the trick is to stay asleep, even though you are awake. I have found the trick to staying asleep while you are awake is to not make a big deal about it. Excitement could wake you up, so be as matter-of-fact about it as you can, and proceed from there. You may wish to just watch the events of the dream unfold without influencing them, or you can make conscious choices about what you want to do in the dream.

The most important attitude to cultivate is your intention to lucid dream. Before sleep, tell yourself that you will remember your dreams, and you will wake up in the dream. You might find it helpful to ask both your superconscious and subconscious selves to wake up your conscious mind. If you wish, you can also ask your spirit guides or teachers to wake you up. If you know you have support in the spirit world, it can make it easier to attain your goal.

Going to sleep as consciously as possible is very beneficial in assisting lucid dream states. As you are drifting off, try to stay conscious enough to reflect on where your mind has been wandering. You may even catch yourself dreaming in the process. A more active technique along these lines is to place yourself in a scene. Make your experience of this place as vivid as possible. Engage all your senses in the experience. As you drift off within your created scene, notice when you are creating the scene and when the scene seems to be creating itself.

Another technique which I have found particularly useful is to repeat to myself, "1…I'm dreaming, 2…I'm dreaming, 3…I'm dreaming, etc.." until I fall asleep. This technique allows you to go directly from the waking state to the lucid dream state. [4] It has worked best for me during daytime naps. In my experience, being well rested definitely is ideal for bringing on lucid dreams. My most vivid dreams have been in the morning after a good night's sleep.

Pick a signal to wake yourself up within the dream. Choose something you can't do in your daily life. I have wakened myself up when dreaming many times by flying. Whenever I find myself flying, I know I must be dreaming.

There are several Tibetan Buddhist dream yoga techniques that I have found to be profoundly helpful. One involves visualizing the Tibetan symbol for the sound "ah-h" in the center of your body. You can also just see it as a white letter "A" if you like. Keep your attention  focused on that sound and that visualization as you drift of to sleep. Keep it there even in your dream state, maintaining the sound and visualization constantly. Chant *ah-h-h* as soon as you awaken in the morning to maintain the continuity. [5]

Another Tibetan dream visualization that you can work with is imagining a beautiful pink lotus with a reddish-orange flame

in its center in your throat chakra. See the edges of the flame as very distinct. Focus on the tip of the flame. The flame in the center represents awareness, while the flower represents consciousness. Focus your awareness in the center to maintain consciousness. You may even wish to draw this image and place in view of your bed as a reminder. [6]

If you wake up remembering a dream, you can try to go back and relive the experience of the dream, only this time, imagine yourself waking up in the dream. Experience it "as if" you are lucid dreaming. This helps to induce lucid dreams when you go back to sleep by accustoming your psyche to lucid dreaming through practice.

Try out these techniques, and see which ones work best for you. If there is one or two that you like, stick with them for a while. Remember, this may not happen overnight. It is important to be persistent with your dream programming. It can take from days to months to reach the desired effect, but the more you do the work, the more effective you will be. The more conscious intent you put into your dream work, the easier it will be to enter the dream state consciously.

It is important to believe in your ability to influence and create your dream reality to make it work. Faith is an important key to altering both waking and dream realities.

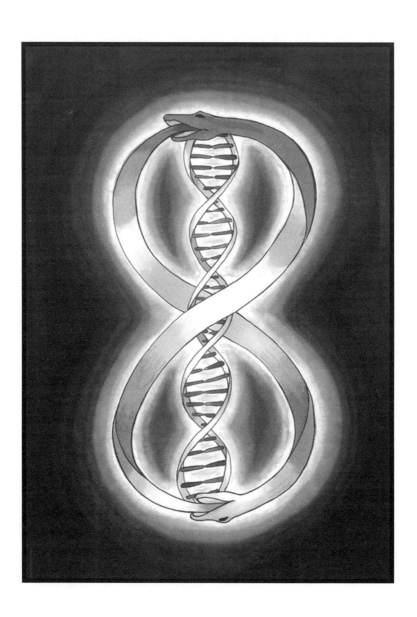

8

Karmic Re-Patterning and the Chakras

The Nature of Karma

In Alchemy, a *double ourobouros* (two serpents swallowing one another) signifies volatility and the potential for change. It also signifies the balance of our upper and lower natures. It looks very much like the number eight, which is the number of responsibility, karma and positive change. The Pythagoreans considered the number eight to signify justice. Karma is a principle that enacts the justice of the cosmos. Karma is synonymous with the law of cause and effect.

Eight holds the possibility of regeneration and resurrection. It represents the prospect for positive change in our lives through the ability to apply ideas and effort effectively. In *8*, we can resolve our thoughts and feelings related to the past and truly come into the present moment where all the magic is.

The DNA double helix looks somewhat like the numeral eight. Spiraling around itself, the DNA holds the genetic coding for physical organisms. It keeps track of everything that has been, and paves the way for everything that will be. Similarly, on a metaphysical level, the akashic records keep track of everything that has ever been and ever will be. The akashic records are not a set of books in some library in the sky. They are contained within the collective knowledge of all creation as a field of consciousness. They can be likened to DNA of the soul beyond time.

Newton's third law of motion states: "For every action, there is an equal and opposite reaction," While Newton likely did not intend to describe karma through the third law of motion, we can use that law as a useful analogy to understand the nature of karma. Simplified, the law of karma states that no matter what you do, it will come back to you at some time or another. We are all inextricably linked with our environment. There is a dynamic relationship between the self and that which surrounds it.

The Laws of karma and Newton's law of motion do seem to differ in some fundamental ways. For example, the effect that occurs is not always exactly opposite to the cause. Often, karma acts more like a loop that repeats the same pattern over and over again until we get the lesson and move on. Nor is karma always equal between its cause and effect. Once someone is able to apply consciousness and get the lesson, the effect is exponentially lessened. Conversely, sometimes we can apply small amounts of effort combined with a positive intent, and reap large rewards.

Through karmic law's natural feedback system, the original action can find completion. This is true for both negative and positive actions. When we cause harm, harm returns to us. When

we perform good actions, we create karmic merit, and move ahead spiritually.

One of the pitfalls with this particular law is that the karmic wheel can sometimes be like a merry (or not-so-merry) go round that we don't know how to get off. For example, if someone hurts you in some way, and then you hurt that person in return, that person gets angry, and then seeks retribution again. This pattern repeats in a cyclical fashion for many lifetimes. It includes many other people, who get hurt on the sidelines as result of the original conflict. These people, in turn, hurt others, who also return the hurt.

As you can see, karma can expand exponentially. This tendency to respond with reaction instead of constructive interaction is one reason things have gotten so nutty on this planet.

How Can We Break These Crazy Cycles?

How do we get out of this mess? It is the responsibility of each of us to not return negative actions with another negative reaction. When we refrain from reacting with more negativity, we can break the cycle that creates more negativity, karma and suffering on the planet. This is no easy task. It requires more courage to be peaceful than it does to fight. Breaking the cycle of action and reaction is the key to re-patterning karmic tendencies.

It is possible to lessen the intensity of the return on our karmic debt by the way in which we approach our lives. If we engage life from a perspective of openness, truth, compassion and love, karma has a way of winding down to less extreme results. For example, if your karma was to be knocked flat by a tree, perhaps you would only have a leaf fall on your head instead. Once we really get the lesson, we can then move on.

Do you have some reoccurring theme in your life? Maybe you choose relationships with people who will ultimately reject you, or find yourself controlled, or controlling. Maybe you are never able to complete projects, you are always trying to find approval from others, or you have a perpetual sense of lack. These are all themes of karmic patterning and they can be broken and transformed into more fulfilling patterns if we are truly willing to embrace change in our lives.

The numeral eight, turned on its side, symbolizes infinity. The infinity symbol is like a *Moebius strip* that has no beginning and no end. Even through our experiences of birth and death, we continue on, immortal and infinite. The point at which the two loops meet can be thought of as a symbol for both birth and death.

Birth and death are inseparable. For everything that dies, something is born anew. The true nature of both birth and death is transition, ultimately becoming transformation. Physical birth and death marks our entry and exit from this earthly plane of existence, but we also experience birth and death on a daily basis in the form of change. When we want to grow and change, we must allow for the death of our old patterns to create new ways of interfacing with life. That point in the wheel of infinity where birth and death meet is the point at which we have the option to change our lives. That point is the eternal now; it is the absolute stillness. We are always at choice in this place, whether or not we choose to be affected by the past and the future.

Sometimes these little deaths can be painful and difficult because they mean we must leave behind what is familiar, even though the pattern, behavior or situation is ultimately detrimental to our well-being. We become addicted to what we already know, often in spite of our intellectual understanding of what would be best for us. It takes a lot of courage to step off into the unknown towards a new way of being. Just as so many of us fear death, we often fear the little deaths that amount to change in our lives. If we are to change, we need to learn how to view this point in the wheel as the point of decision where we are able to choose new life and possibility over slavery to habitual patterns.

Creating conscious change takes clear intent and strong will power. It requires that we override our internal programming, slowly wearing away our ingrained concepts of self; similar to the way a river wears down rock in a streambed. Constant reminders, daily meditative practices, the practice of mindfulness, and focused healing work often are all necessary to clear out lifetimes of negative thought processes. Steadfastly inviting positive change in our lives is the path of the spiritual warrior, one who is willing to take on the demons of the self for spiritual, emotional, mental, and physical liberation. The path of the shaman is to welcome death in order to experience rebirth.

If we want a larger life, a freer life, or a more harmonious life, we need to move beyond the habitual patterns we have become accustomed to. This is challenging, because it automatically means moving outside the comfort zone of the familiar. The first step is to see the pattern. The second step is to make a different choice. The third is acting on the choice. The fourth, and often most difficult step, is to maintain that choice in the face of habitual patterns, until the habit of the negative conditioning is broken.

The Origins of Karma

To effectively deal with karmic patterns, we must look at their origins. All karmic patterns are based in events that have shaped our world view. The roots of karmic patterning can be based in seemingly inconsequential messages from childhood that have gained strength over time, or from the major traumatic events that are more obvious influences on our lives. Sometimes the roots of karmic patterning are hidden from view because the origins of the pattern exist in another lifetime. We can experience "bleed through" from other lives, recreating similar patterning in this life without knowing why.

Often enough, it is unnecessary to dig up information from other lifetimes. Usually there is enough material available from the lifetime you are in to illustrate your basic karmic patterns so that you can figure out what you need to work on. You recreate reflections of your soul's journey in every lifetime. Every lifetime is a microcosm of the macrocosm. The whole is reflected in all of its parts, not unlike a *fractal pattern*, which expands and multiplies based on the root pattern.

Trauma and Cellular Memory

When we experience trauma, our natural inclination is to try to stop action by holding our breath. This reflexive action actually cements the trauma into our cellular memory. In effect, we do not allow the situation to pass through us. By resisting the situation, and resisting "surrendering to the moment," we prolong our agony. The old adage, "What we resist, persists." applies quite well here.

Trauma combined with resistance creates blockage in the cellular memory. When this happens, a crystallization process occurs that makes us denser energetically. In this dense state, it becomes more difficult to perceive reality in terms of light and energy. For this reason, if we wish to grow spiritually so that we may perceive and experience reality from these more subtle levels, it is essential that we work to heal on all levels. Spiritual growth is inseparable from emotional and psychological growth.

This "crystallization" within the cells is also the root of disease. Physical illness is the most dense symptom of some root pattern that we are holding. Illness is the outcome of our karmic patterning. It is the soul's way of saying "Pay attention to this." All illness can be traced back to the incorrect assumptions about the nature of reality that we came up with based on our experiences in life. Negative emotional states arising from those wrong assumptions, such as anger, fear, grief, guilt, shame, rejection, and hatred cause even more damage. Even genetically caused illness can be linked to the crystallization of trauma within genetically inherited DNA, as well as through self concepts that were passed down to us by our parents and our parent's parents.

A powerful tool for breaking up the crystallization within the cellular memory is breath work. Conscious breathing techniques hyper-oxygenate the cells, breaking up the density of karmic patterning. Certain breathing techniques can bring memories and /or patterns created by traumatic experiences to the surface to be released and healed. Breath work can transform the initial resistance we experienced at the root of our traumas into movement and healing.

Visualization and affirmations are also effective tools for changing our perceptions and ultimately, our experience of life. By visualizing and affirming our world and ourselves as healed, loved, nurtured, and abundant, we alter the path of destiny towards wholeness for all creation. Thought has power. When these tools are used in conjunction with breath, the results are often much more powerful. By engaging the body, mind and heart simultaneously, transformation is imminent. In this chapter, we will be dealing specifically with breath and visualization techniques, as well as affirmations that can help to shift karmic patterning.

Some Differing Notions about Chakras

Working with the chakras is a profound way to effect change and healing. The chakras are energy vortexes that exist within the subtle body. In Sanskrit, the word chakra means "wheel." The chakras can be visualized as wheels of energy. Each chakra represents a different aspect of our experience as human beings. By working with the energies of the chakras, it is possible to create inner balance and clear away the blockages and negativity that prevent us from becoming healed whole beings in alignment with our highest nature.

There are several different spiritual systems that work with these energy vortexes. The most widely used Hindu system utilizes seven chakras, though in more obscured Hindu texts, there are other chakras described in the subtle body in or above the head. Different colors are ascribed to the different chakras for visualization and vibrational purposes. Varied Hindu sources use different color systems to describe the different chakras. The Tibetan paradigm uses a five chakra system with some secondary chakras. In some Buddhist traditions, the only center focused on is the *hara*, in the pit of the belly.

All these systems have an overlapping quality of similarity, yet each is unique in its approach. No one system is the *right* system. You yourself must determine what system feels right for you.

I'm including this information to illustrate the point that there are multitudes of ways to perceive and do things. If something works for someone, they should by all means do it even if it doesn't mesh with another person's concept of "right." I would suggest though, that if you do work with a particular chakra system, you stick with it if it's working, because the focus of your attention and intention on visualizing and experiencing a particular system will tend to anchor that energetic system in your body, mind and psyche. Anchoring several energetic systems could get confusing and cloud your development of a clear personal symbology system. Do what feels right for you. Everyone must follow his or her own path of inner guidance. In this book, I will be focusing on an elaboration on the most commonly known Hindu seven chakra system.

Chakra Descriptions

These chakra descriptions include the positions of the chakras, each chakra's essential nature, and the colors and visual symbols, or *yantras* associated with them.

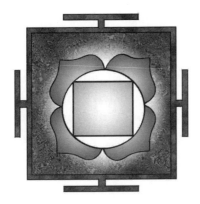

Root Chakra

The base or root chakra is located several inches into the body from the perineum, between the anus and the genitals. It is represented by the color red. The drive associated with this chakra is the will to survive. In the first chakra we must learn to balance our ability to reason with our animal instinct of fight or flight. This means learning to respond appropriately instead of reacting without proper forethought to experiences that occur in your life. Our primal fear is processed in the root chakra. Issues around abundance and security also work themselves out in this center. The element associated with the chakra is earth. The sense is smell. The Sanskrit name for this chakra is *Muladhara*.

Sex Chakra

The second chakra is located around four finger widths below the navel. This center is represented by the color orange. The drive associated with this chakra is self-gratification. It is the center of our sexual energy, pleasure and the emotions. Guilt, shame and issues regarding sexuality are stored and resolved

in this center. The element associated with the chakra is water. The sense is taste. The Sanskrit name for this chakra is *Swadhisthana*.

Solar Plexus Chakra

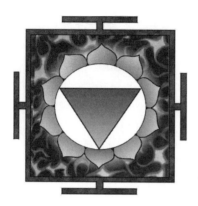

The third chakra is located in the solar plexus. The color that represents this chakra is yellow. Self-definition is the drive associated with this center. It is the seat of our personal will. Issues around personal power and control are centered in this chakra. This is the center in which we cram, and eventually heal, many of our repressed feelings of anxiety and anger. The element associated with the chakra is fire. The sense is sight. The Sanskrit name for this chakra is *Manipura*.

Heart Chakra

The fourth chakra is located in the heart. The heart chakra is represented by the color green. Self-acceptance is the driving force associated with this center. It is the center that connects the lower chakras with the upper chakras, spirit with matter, and your being with all other beings.

The heart chakra represents the oneness with all that is, expressed through compassion and caring. Issues in the heart mainly are centered in feeling as though we are somehow separate from others or from the Divine. Grief and loneliness are processed in the heart chakra.

Excessive focus on the mind and logical thought, doubt and skepticism, ownership and attachment all can cause blockages in this center. Love cannot be truly understood; it can only be felt.

It cannot be owned; it can only be shared. Love requires and inspires trust. The element associated with the chakra is air. The sense is touch. The Sanskrit name for this chakra is *Anahata*.

Throat Chakra

The fifth chakra is located at the base of the throat. Blue is the color associated with this center. The driving force associated with this center is communication and expression. It is from this center that we express our thoughts, ideas, feelings, needs, and desires. When we do not truthfully and fully express ourselves, this chakra can become blocked. The throat chakra is also the center for our "inner ear," or clairaudience. Clairaudience is the ability to hear messages from the Divine. The element associated with the chakra is ether. The sense is hearing. The Sanskrit name for this chakra is *Vishuddhi*.

Third Eye Chakra

The sixth chakra is located in the middle of the forehead and is often referred to as the "third eye." The color that represents this chakra is indigo. The driving force behind this center is the desire to understand. The third eye is the center where knowledge of spirit becomes accessible to the conscious mind. It is in this center that our intuition blossoms, and we receive the ability to clairvoyantly "see" into the various realms to bring back wisdom to share and integrate into the third dimensional reality. This is the center for visual psychic skills such as the reading of auras (energy around the body), seeing the chakras, seeing through time and space, shamanic journeying, and prophetic and spirit dreaming. It is considered to be the 'command center' for all of the lower chakras, as the ida, pingala and sushumna channels come to a confluence there. The Sanskrit name for this chakra is *Ajna*.

Crown Chakra

The seventh chakra is at the top of the head and is often referred to as the crown chakra. Violet is the color associated with this center. The driving force of this chakra is to ascend. It is in this center that we truly learn how to integrate with the Divine. In the seventh chakra, we dissolve our little egos into the oneness with the cosmos. It is the center for divine imagination and our place of illumination. The Sanskrit name for this chakra is *Sahasrara*.

Feet and Hand Chakras

Two additional centers I'd like to mention are in the soles of the feet and in the palms of the hands. The energetic centers in the feet connect us to the Earth, and our path and life's work on the Earth. When these centers are blocked, we may experience feeling "ungrounded," or uncertain of what we're doing or why we're here. Blockages may also create an inability to "stand up for ourselves" or to be self-reliant.

The energetic centers in the hands assist us in the powers of self-expression and the channeling of psychic energy. They can also act as energetic sensors to perceive energetic realities. Hands-on healers rely heavily on these centers to perceive the health and well being of their patients, and to transmit energy from the cosmos to their patients for healing.

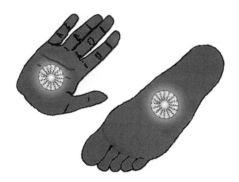

Chakra Meditation

Lie down or sit cross-legged in a comfortable place where you will not be disturbed for the duration of the meditation. Get comfortable and relax. Take a few deep breaths. Inhale and exhale. Take your time and really experience you breath, in.... and out.... Feel your body connecting with the ground below you. Imagine the magnetic force of the Earth as the embrace of Mother Earth. Imagine the magnetic force as the attracting force of love. It is a loving embrace from the Earth. Feel your self sinking deeper and deeper into the ground beneath you. Be aware of every part of your body, merging more and more with the energy of the Earth. Completely relax, and allow your self to let go into deeper and deeper levels of your psyche.

Now, be aware of your body in the first chakra in the area just above the perineum. Be aware of the physical sensations here. Imagine that you can move energy in and out of this place with your inhalation, and exhalation. Move energy in and out of the first chakra with the breath. See the root chakra as being a brilliant red color. With every inhalation of your breath, see and feel that red color becoming brighter and clearer, and with every exhalation allow dark colors or blocked energy to be released. Give the blocked energy over to the Earth to be transformed back into pure energy. Allow the magnetic force of the Earth draw blocked energy from you. Surrender to the flow. While breathing in, allow light and healing to flow into you. As you exhale, release old blocked energy patterns. Feel yourself becoming more and more present and grounded with every breath.

Repeat these affirmations with inner strength and conviction. Anchor these affirmations in your first chakra.

The Universe provides for me and protects me.
I am completely at ease in my body, and on the Earth.
I am an immortal soul.
I am safe.

On your next inhalation, take a deep breath, and pull your awareness of the energy up to the second chakra, about four finger widths below your navel. Be aware of all physical sensations in this area. Imagine you are breathing energy in and out of this center. Imagine the breath as the pure energy of the universe filling this chakra. Inhale deeply, and exhale deeply. As you breathe in, visualize a brilliant orange colored light in your second chakra, growing and becoming brighter. As you exhale, release the dark colors, blocked energy or negative thoughts you have about your self that are being held in this center. Release any pain you may have around your experience of being a man or woman, and about your sexuality. Just let it go, you don't need it any more. Draw in the light, and release the dark. Give and receive from the Earth, and from the universe. Allow balance to fill this center.

Repeat these affirmations with inner strength and conviction. Anchor them in your second chakra.

My sexuality is sacred.
I deserve pleasure.
The creative force of the Universe
expresses itself through me.

On your next inhalation, move your awareness up to the third chakra, into your solar plexus. Feel the sensations in this part of your body. Breathe deeply in and out of this center. Breathe in the vital force of the universe on the inhalation, and visualize a vibrant yellow light growing very bright in this center. When you exhale, release the blocked energies, dark colors and negative patterns you have held in this place. Breathe in and fill with life force, breathe out and release what is not needed. Your will is aligning with the Divine will with every inward breath. With every exhalation, release your need to control, and any fear about being controlled.

Repeat these affirmations with inner strength and conviction. Anchor them in your third chakra.

I am the creator of my own destiny
I know who I am, and what I want to choose
My will, and the Divine will are one.

On your next inhalation, move your awareness up to the fourth chakra, to your heart. Breathe in and out of this center. Experience the physical sensations of this area. Breathe in and out of your heart chakra. Imagine the breath as the love of the universe flowing into you as you inhale. When you exhale, release loneliness, grief and fear of loss out of this place. Visualize a beautiful emerald green light filling your whole chest on your inhale, and release the darkness on the exhale. Feel yourself opening and allowing more love into your life with every breath. Feel yourself as being connected to all beings. Know that you are never alone.

Repeat these affirmations with inner strength and conviction. Anchor them in your heart chakra.

I open my heart and feel deeply.
Through the power of love, I am connected to everything.
Compassion flows to me from the Universe,
and compassion flows from me to all that is.
I am love.

On your next inhalation, move your awareness up to your throat chakra. Be aware of the physical sensations in your throat. Visualize a bright blue light in this place that grows in strength as you breathe in. On the exhale release any blocked energy that you might feel there. Free all unexpressed words and feelings that need to let go. Breathe light and energy in, and when you exhale, make sound to help you to open your throat and release the energy there. Let the sounds be representative of all the words you never got to say, or never allowed yourself to say. Let the sounds express your creative flow. Let the sounds express your emotions.

Repeat these affirmations with inner strength and conviction. Anchor them in your throat chakra.

I express myself clearly and completely.
I deserve to be heard.
The Divine speaks to me and through me.

On the next inhalation, move your awareness up to your brow chakra. Feel the physical sensations of this area. Imagine you are breathing in and out of your third eye. Visualize an indigo light that grows more brilliant with every inhalation. Release any blocked energy of this place on the exhalation. With every breath, feel yourself opening more and more to the Divine intelligence of the Universe. Imagine that each breath assists you in opening your third eye, and freeing up your inner vision. Allow that divine wisdom to fill you.

Repeat these affirmations with inner strength and conviction. Anchor them in your brow chakra.

Divine wisdom flows through me.
Truth and clarity fill my visions.
The mystery of Spirit reveals itself to me everyday.

On the next breath, move your awareness up to your crown chakra, at the top of your head. Be aware of the physical sensations you feel there. See a violet light on the top of your head. Imagine you are breathing in and out of this place. On the inhalation, fill your crown chakra with light and energy. On the exhalation, release any blocked energy that might be held there. Imagine you have a lotus bud on your head. With every breath, see and feel the lotus opening, petal by petal into a beautiful flower. As this chakra opens, see your connection to Spirit grow stronger. Feel your limited self-concept dissolve into the limitlessness of the Divine.

Repeat these affirmations with inner strength and conviction. Anchor them in your crown chakra.

> *Illumination fills my being.*
> *I am light.*
> *The Divine and I are One.*
> *I am.*

Now breathe in your first chakra, and draw the energy up through all of your chakras in one breath. Visualize the colors each chakra from base to crown, as if you are breathing in a rainbow. On the exhalation, send the energy out the top of your head, and then allow the energy to fall around you like a rainbow fountain. Return your consciousness to the base chakra. Repeat the process, inhaling once again. Breath in the rainbow, breathe in the totality of who you are. Let the breath and the energy connect and unite the energy vortexes of your chakras. See the colors of your chakras as bright and luminous.

Repeat these affirmations with strength and conviction. Anchor them throughout your body.

> *I am vibrantly alive.*
> *I am fully present, here and now.*
> *All parts of myself work together to create perfect harmony.*

Visualize a silver egg of luminous silver energy around you. See this lunar energy grow stronger and brighter with every inhalation. With every exhalation, see it expand and grow stronger. Imagine you are completely surrounded by the silver energy. Breathe deeply and fully. Imagine you are in a silvery womb of energy, which helps you to love and care for yourself more fully.

Now visualize a luminous egg of gold light around the silver one. With every inhalation, see this solar light grow stronger and brighter. With every exhalation, see it expand and grow brighter. See the gold light completely encompassing you.

See all the love, abundance, wisdom, and peace you need in your life drawn to you through the gold light. See and feel how this golden shield easily deflects negative or disruptive energies. Breathe, and know that you are protected, and your energy body is sealed with light.

Repeat these affirmations with strength and conviction. Anchor them throughout your light body.

I am shielded, nurtured and protected by a cocoon of light.
I am seated in the heart of the Divine.
I know my relationship to all that is.

Visualize a bright white light above your head. As you breathe, imagine the brightest, whitest light you can possibly imagine. See and feel it growing in size and power. Imagine this as the seat of your high self, and the place from which you manifest your life.

As you breathe, visualize your life unfolding in beauty, aligned with the Divine, surrounded by white light. See and feel yourself receiving all you need to be fulfilled in present time. See yourself sharing the blessings of your life with all creation. Breathe the white light and your vision into your body. Let it fill you.

Repeat these affirmations with strength and conviction. Anchor them throughout your light body and your physical body:

I manifest my life in beauty.
I am completely connected to the Divine flow.
Everything is as it should be.

Working with Kundalini Energy

Kundalini is the dynamic energy force that lives in the spine. This energy lies dormant at the base of the spine until awakened. Within the Hindu system, this dormant energy is thought of as a coiled serpent. It is the feminine force represented by the goddess Shakti.

When awakened, Shakti moves up the spine, opening all the energy centers. Some of the most common ways in which Shakti is awakened are through breath and visualization techniques, meditation, dance, and love making.

Sometimes when people work with breath and the chakras, they experience rushes of energy moving up the spine. This is a  normal symptom of awakening kundalini. When the Shakti is moving you might experience spontaneous outpourings of emotion, bliss-like states, movement of the body to postures or poses, and arm or hand gestures.

Occasionally, people experience twitching or cramping of the hands and feet. These symptoms are due to energy moving through areas in which there is blockage and resistance. If this ever happens to you, just relax and let the energy do the work.

Working with kundalini is the most powerful tool for transformation that I know of. It awakens you to, and will move you through, any blockages you may have in a very direct fashion. If you chose to work with kundalini in a very intentional way, you will be asked to confront your own inner darkness and move through your pain, as well as release into the bliss of spirit. Working with kundalini is not for the faint of heart. It has a tendency to open the Pandora's box of the soul. It will definitely help you to discern and move through any karmic patterns you may have. Working with kundalini Shakti is a commitment to change.

Shakti's counterpart is Shiva. The Shiva current runs from the top of the head, down to the root chakra. The Shiva energy is the deep stillness of awakened awareness. When we work with Shakti and Shiva together, the primal energy is brought to the crown to transform our baser aspects and energies. It merges with the Shiva energy in the head, and then the Shiva energy descends down the spine, bringing awakened awareness to the unconscious aspects of the psyche.

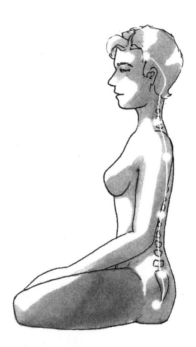

Spinal Breathing Meditation

It is especially good to do the spinal breathing after performing the chakra meditation. The chakra meditation will center you and clear the way to move the Shakti-Shiva energy through your body in a full circuit. In this meditation, we will be moving the energy up the spine through the spinal nerve to the third eye chakra on the inhalation, and then release the energy back down the spine to the first chakra on the exhalation. Here is a diagram of the path the energy takes in this exercise.

Rest the underside of your tongue on the roof of your mouth. This creates a connection in your energetic circuitry for the vital force to flow through. Visualize a transparent tube running up the inside of spine to the center of your brain where ajna chakra resides. Imagine that the chakras are like jewels strung upon this thread. Focus on the first chakra. As you inhale, imagine luminous steaks of white light rising up from the first chakra through the transparent tube, through each of the chakras to where the spine meets the skull. The energy then enters your head and rises to ajna chakra in the center of the brain, all in one inhalation. Hold the energy and your awareness at ajna chakra while you hold your breath. Imagine light emanating from ajna chakra, illuminating and awakening your crown chakra. Release the breath, and allow the energy to flow back down the spine to the first chakra. Think of your chakras as "train stops" along the way as you breath your awareness up and down the channel. Don't pause at the chakras as you pass through them. Just feel and acknowledge them as you go by. Repeat this exercise for a little while.

At the completion of this breath meditation, return your energy and awareness to the root chakra. This will help to integrate the spiritualizing force into your body and into the physical plane. To ground your energy, be aware of your connection to the Earth. Feel the magnetic force grounding you. You can imagine roots growing down from your base into the Earth. Feel your core energy, and breathe deeply. You may then want to lie down, so you can feel the Earth energy in contact with your whole body. Take some time to relax in silent meditation, allowing the energy and your consciousness to do what it needs to do in order to integrate the energy from the meditation. You can begin by doing this exercise 3-5 minutes a day. Over time, you may gradually increase the length of time if you like.

9

Art and Spirituality

Through the number nine, we can synthesize and harmonize with the energies of all of the other numbers through our creativity. The creative process is a profound means for us to actualize that deep integration. Once we have integrated our realizations through the creative process, we can then share those gifts with others.

The number nine is also the number of the humanitarian, one who is broad-minded, compassionate, one who thinks universally, and generously gives to the community. With the creative process, one cannot help but share the riches, as art is often a communal event that is shared with others.

Nine is a number of passion, emotion and extreme feelings, which may be easily shared through the creative arts. It is the number of attainment, maximum intensity and complete fulfillment.

Art, by its nature, has an intensity to it. When we are being deeply creative, we dip into the deep well of our soul and bring forth the riches in the language of the Infinite. Nine is the number of all possibilities that may be realized when we apply our creativity to the expression of our potential.

The Muses

In Greco-Roman mythology, there are nine muses that are the representatives of poetry, the arts and sciences. Each of the muses has her own creative domain. Calliope is the muse of epic song and philosophy. Clio is the muse of history and heroic poetry. Euterpe is the muse of lyric song. Thalia is the muse of comedy and poetry. Melpomene is the muse of tragedy. Terpsichore is the muse of dance. Erato is the muse of erotic and love poetry. Polyhymnia is the muse of sacred song, and Urania is the muse of astronomy, astrology and Universal love. When Pythagoras arrived at Croton, his first advice to the people who lived there was to build a shrine to the Muses at the center of the city to promote civic harmony and learning.

The muses love to express themselves through the creative impulse and share that gift with others. They allow the creative forces of the universe to work through them. Mythologically speaking, the muses would mainly perform and create for the Gods. The muses are alive and well, flourishing in the expression of our own art. They represent the Divine inspiration that fuels the creative process for each one of us.[1]

Art and Spirituality

There is a profound connection between art and spirituality. When a person is engaging in an artistic endeavor, they are participating in an act of creation. In that moment of creation there is a natural connection between the artist and the Creator of all that is. In essence, the artist becomes  the Creator. One of the reasons why we are here on Earth is to participate in the ongoing creative process of the universe. We are aspects of the Divine and we expand the wisdom and experience of the Cosmic Creator through our own creative process.

Art is a way of approaching life, not just the expression of artistic skills. The experience of the act of creativity and its relationship to the Divine is not only for those who describe themselves as artists. One can experience the beauty of creation through performing any creative act.

If you are someone who does not consider yourself artistically inclined, know that this chapter is also for you. It might require some creative transposition to think about this material as it relates to your own creative process. We all have access to the experience of the creative whether it is in cooking, designing something, creating beauty through order, or any other creative process. What is your creative passion?

When we are deep in the creative process we enter a world of our own; it is as if nothing else exists except for the stroke of the brush, the movement of the arm, or the musical line being played. It is a complete immersion, a fusion with the art itself. In this fusion, we can lose our sense of the ego, or individuated self, and merge with something larger. In merging with this great force, profound healing is possible.

In the artistic process, it is as though we enter a reality or dimension where all possibility exists. We take the raw materials of paper, clay, musical instruments, whatever our media might be, and combine that with the little or great skills that we have. We apply our time and attention, and *voilà!* The masterpiece is brought to manifestation. What is created is not any one of these things but something greater that is beyond the sum of its parts.

Within the creative process, when the linear and liminal meet and communicate, we enter a creative zone where our personality and ego-awareness are lost in the act of doing. In that loss of ego-self we are merged into the divine and refined by it. Many artists find that their best art happens in this state. It can feel almost like flying or surfing on a wave of the creative force, and it is a high like none other!

Beauty, Truth, Art, and Spirit

Part of the beauty of the creative process is the expression or experience of beauty and truth. Much of art is an expression of what we consider beautiful or important. Through art we can appreciate the beauty in the universe whether it is a representation of something in the world we find beautiful, in the elegance of a movement in a dance, or in the interplay of colors in a painting. Our appreciation of beauty awakens within us an inner experience of appreciation. Whether or not you are the creator or the witness to the creation, the appreciation of beauty brings you closer to that experience of the Divine.

Similarly, the process of creativity, whether it is being expressed or witnessed, often engages a person's sense of truth as well. For example, there are some forms of art that people may not consider to be beautiful, but somehow that art engages in them an emotional reaction that brings them closer to their concept of what is true. That expression or the freedom to express that truth contains its own sort of beauty.

In the movie *Mona Lisa Smile,* Julia Roberts' character is an art teacher in university. She has her students looking at a piece of art by the American abstract-expressionist painter Jackson Pollock, who was famous for the art he produced in the 1940's and the 1950's. She teaches her students that they are not required to like or love the piece. What they are required to do is to consider it. There is a great wisdom in this. The appreciation of art not only relates to its potential for beauty or the personal resonance one might experience in relation to it but also for its potential to broaden our minds and our perspective. Art opens our minds to broader expressions of possibility, exposing us to the many possibilities for understanding and appreciating human experience as expressed through art. When we do experience that profound resonance with a piece of art, dance or music, it connects us with our ability to feel, remember or experience something that brings us home to ourselves in a new way.

Creativity, The Spiritual Language that Unifies Us

As diverse as humanity is, art has the potential to be a unifying force. Much of art has the ability to transcend linguistic and cultural barriers. While cultures throughout the world are extremely diverse, the human experience is still relatively consistent. We are born and we grow up. We have gains and losses, happiness, sadness, failures and successes. We live our lives and then we pass beyond this world.

Our art expresses our most ancient archetypes that are shared by the human community. While the symbols may have some variation, the archetypes are often consistent. In the expression of archetypal imagery through art, we can catch a glimpse of the world from artists who have never communicated or seen each other's art. This consistency of archetypes shows the transcendent nature of art and how it goes beyond the assumed boundaries that appear to separate people.

One time I was listening to Sami Shaman Ailu Gaup talk about creativity. We had just finished doing some shamanic journey work, and he encouraged us to express our experience through poetry or through pictures. He felt that because symbolic imagery is the language of the psyche, this was the most effective way to communicate the experience of the journey.

When we express ourselves from this deeply creative place, we can more deeply engage and express the experiences of the inner self. While words can limit the full expression of an experience, the symbolic language of art gives us a wider palette to draw from. By expressing the journey through art and or poetry, we help to keep the right-brained perspective of the spiritual experience intact as we attempt to convey and record the experience. When we try to qualify and quantify our experience through a linear recitation of events, something is likely to get lost. By reiterating the experience through poetry and art, more of the essence or the *feel* of the experience is kept intact.

When we express the experience of our psyches through the creation of art, we make a profound connection between the subconscious realm of the inner dreamer and the conscious self. The very act of making art is a Divine union of the conscious and subconscious minds. In that union, we hold the potential to come into a place of inner harmony and in the moment of that union we have the opportunity to capture a glimpse of the Divine as it manifests through us.

As we discussed in Chapter 2, the balancing of our hemispheres is a part of what brings about an enlightened state through tantric means. Art can be an amazing tantric exercise in balancing these aspects of ourselves.

Performing or creating art can create a connection between the two halves of the brain. The left side of the brain provides the small motor skills and the required intellectual capacity to operate the media required to create the art. The right side of the brain is the part of our mind that makes the intuitive leaps necessary for new ideas and art to occur. This intuitive aspect of the right brain fathoms reality beyond the mundane world of existence and provides the inspiration needed to make art. In all great art, both the linear and relational aspects of our selves are required. In the creation of art, these two parts of us are conjoined in balance to bring about something awe-inspiring.

Art is one way in which we can connect to Jung's *collective unconscious*, which is the great well of archetypal imagery that we share as a species. The language of the collective unconscious is spoken in symbol. Art is the natural media of symbol, expressed in creativity's many forms. The collective unconscious is like a river that is flowing. It is always changing and evolving. This field of consciousness is not only the group mind of humanity. It is also a part of the spiritual potential of the whole universe. The artist taps into the flow of that river and channels it up into the light of consciousness. The information from that field of consciousness helps to facilitate change within the entire human experience. Often when the artist is engaged in the process, it can feel as though he or she is personally expressing something larger than life. Artists are the priestesses and priests of change.

In aboriginal societies, the priest and priestess are almost always artists because there is a natural connection between the two. The artist channels spiritual forces and the flow of change within the collective. We can think of the artist as a conduit for spiritual and evolutionary change; moreover, the artist is a mediator between the source and the receiver. The artist can be like a lens that brings ideas and emotions into a sharper focus. Artists give us a gift: the gift of being able to see, to feel, to hear the artists' experience through their eyes, their ears, and the movement of the energy through their bodies. That is a deep magic.

Art and Non-Ordinary Reality

The creative process can bring the artist into connection with non-ordinary reality. In non-ordinary reality, we are connected to a deep well of energy and inspiration that can be conducted and channeled for our own healing and for the healing of others. In the artistic process, it is easy to enter a trance state in which the energies of spirit and healing can easily penetrate in order to create positive transformation. Art not only gives us the opportunity to connect with these divine energies. Ultimately it gives us opportunities for transcendence and transformation.

In the creative process we also have the opportunity to drop into a liminal space where time has no meaning. We are both that which is being done and the doer. We tap into what is, what was and what will be, merging in and beyond time.

Creativity as Healer

Creativity is a powerful healer. There was a ground-breaking study involving drumming performed at Meadville Medical Center by a team of MD's using control groups and blood tests, led by researcher, author and cancer expert Barry Bittman, MD. The study showed that group drumming increases cancer-killing cells that help the body combat not only cancer but also other viruses such as AIDS. [2]

Endorphins and other neurochemicals are also released when we concentrate deeply on our creative process. Brain waves from deep creative concentration and meditation have been shown to look very similar. In that brain wave state, heart rate is lowered, and blood pressure drops, creating a relaxation response that is extremely beneficial to health. [3]

Through the creative process we can engage deeper aspects of ourselves that are beyond the linear mind. In this state of engagement, these deeper parts of the psyche are able to express themselves, bringing about transformation. By diving into the depths through art, we can not only connect with the ecstatic parts of ourselves, we can also connect with the shadow aspects of ourselves that seek resolve. By giving the shadow aspect of ourselves a voice, it sets that part of us free to become something new, to be reforged and transformed into something of worth and beauty.

You can see much evidence of this process in music and in writing. How many great works of art have been forged out of a place of sadness, despair, grief and anger?

The soul gets a lot of healing accomplished in the process of expression. When we can expose our difficult experiences to the light of day through artistic expression, it gives us an opportunity to reposition ourselves in relation to our emotions and to our past experiences.

That expression assists in a process of creating resolve. I notice that when I complete a piece of art, I feel a sense of both artistic completion and spiritual completion.

Art as the Expression of Essence

In the artistic process we have the opportunity to express concepts through our skill with the media we are working in. In addition, we have the opportunity to experience and express our own personal essence.

The making of art is a journey of the soul. The artist can discover herself and free her spirit to flow through both the experience and the piece being created. In this way, the art that is created is, in some way, a snapshot of the essence of the artist as it is expressed through the art. For some, art is a shot at immortality. The artist lives on in his art long after the soul has passed on to other realms.

A person experiencing art has the potential to experience some of what the artist might have felt while creating it. The spectator of the art may or may not understand exactly what the artist meant to convey.

Regardless, that person's own psyche will take from the piece what it needs to experience. Works of art that speak to us can touch a place that we might have forgotten existed.

Art can be a touchstone bringing us home to a state of wonder. It can help to reconnect us to our own passions and our desire to express ourselves.

When we share our art work, we share a part of our inner self with the rest of the world and thus contribute to the fullness of human experience.

The Experience of Excellence and The Ecstasy of Riding the Wave

If you are someone who is a more accomplished artist you have probably had the profound experience of being completely in the ecstasy of experiencing your artistic excellence. When you are beginning to learn an artistic modality of some kind, it usually feels pretty clunky because you are still learning the mastery of the brush, paint, word, or instrument. Once you have learned your media well enough so that you can get your intellect out of the way, that is when an amazing door of opportunity opens. The creativity can then begin to flow through on a new level because all the attention and effort is not going to mastery of the media. You can then flow into creating something so much greater than the interaction of persona and the media.

In order to experience the creative process as a spiritual process, it is not necessary to be adept at your art, but it can be extremely helpful. When I am trying to think about how to do something, my attention and my energy are going to the intellectual process. An essential ingredient to reaching that ecstatic state in the creative process is to be able to get the head out of the way. This can be achieved either with or without a high skill level. One of the ways to get the head out of the way is to achieve a level of mastery that puts you beyond it, and the other is to just not worry about whether it meets some standard of excellence.

Dance as a Spiritual Path

Many cultures have used dance as a path to spiritual union. Sufi dervishes spin on and on to experience a sense of unity with all that is. Practitioners of Orisha worship invite the deities to dance through them. In Bali the Sanghyang trance dances are performed to spiritually protect and clear the village. Through dance, it is possible to move beyond the limited perspective of the persona and experience something greater moving in and through us when the ego mind gets out of the way.

Much of what could be considered spiritual dance in modern society we now refer to as *trance dance*. The experience of trance dance requires releasing concern about looking good and focusing on the internal experience of sensation. When we can drop purely into sensation and allow the movement to come from an authentic place, the wisdom of the body is able to express itself more fully. This creates a remarkably powerful opportunity to drop into a deep state of trance meditation.

So much of our expression has been limited by our ideas of what is acceptable or beautiful to others, but that type of dance is ego-focused. When we are focused on the ego, it is more difficult to attain liberation. If we can allow ourselves true freedom of expression and move for the joy of self-expression, it is possible to move into these deeper states.

Movement can be extremely therapeutic for the body, the emotions and the soul. When we move our bodies vigorously over a period of time, endorphins are released as a result of that movement. Those endorphins bring the mind into an altered state. In this altered state, we can move beyond the limitations that have bound us.

Dance is also an opportunity to express the emotions that have been locked within the body energetic. Any experience that we have had that was painful is likely to be held in a static state within the body energetic. When our lungs are pumping and our bodies are moving, we can focus our attention on sensation and emotions within the body. We can use the movement as a vehicle to release the static energy that has been lodged within the body from past trauma.

Wherever we have fear, grief, anger, or any of what we might term "negative or stuck emotions," we have an incredible store of energy. Through accessing those states within the context of movement, we can transform them to pure energy that we can use to make our lives better. When those emotions are released from the body, we are free to live a more unlimited life. When we transform these lower vibration energies through movement, it is possible to experience profound states of ecstasy and release.

Dance and the Path of Ecstasy
Exercise 1: Dance

• Find a piece of music or several pieces of music that make you want to move. Ideally, it should be music that is more instrumentally based without a lot of words so that you are not distracted by the lyrics.

• Have a piece of paper and a pen ready for when you finish.

• Before you turn the music on, notice your thoughts as they pass through your mind, letting them flow on by. Be aware of the sensations of your body, from the top of your head to the tips of your toes. Be aware of your emotions. How you are feeling right in this moment, and how you have been feeling recently in general?

• Take some more deep breaths and bring your awareness into an experience of your essence.

• Turn on the music and allow your movement to originate from your body. Let your body decide how it wants to move, releasing all judgment about appearance. Focus solely on the experience of the movement.

• When you are moving, you can let your movement be inspired by the music, or you can transcend the music and just allow the sensation and emotion to decide the quality of the movement. There is no 'right' way to do this exercise. Allow it to be whatever it is for you. You might find it easier to do if your eyes are either closed or partially closed so that your attention is primarily inward.

• Some important touchstones in your dance will be sensation and emotion. If you find yourself thinking about something outside of sensation and emotion, gently bring yourself back to those experiences.

• Remember to breathe deeply as you move.

• If you feel you want to make sound while you are moving, you can do that as well.

• After the music ends, take a little time in silence to pay attention to how you feel. You might want to compare how you felt when you first started to how you feel after moving.

• Now, take out the paper and pen and draw, journal, or write some poetry about the experience as a way of integrating and anchoring the experience in your psyche.

You might also want to try doing this exercise for an extended period of time and see what happens. Another element you might consider adding is to transform it into a witness-based process. In the witness-based process, one person dances with her attention focused inward while the other person sits on the sidelines and witnesses. The witness' job is not to judge or to analyze but to hold space for the dancer while simultaneously being aware of how she feels when she witnesses this dance. When the dance is complete, the dancer can share her experience with the witness and the witness can share her experience with the dancer. Then they can change places, the witness becomes the dancer and the dancer becomes the witness.

One of the powerful things that can happen in the witness-based process is that when someone is holding space for us as we are dancing, it helps to hold a sacred container for our own transformation. What you might find is that when you do the dance with a witness, your own experience and energy will often feel amplified by the power of that person's attention and intention. You will find that your own ability to be a witness for yourself is also amplified.

Some other exercises you might try are:

• Use dance as a prayer, a means of expressing your connection to the Divine force.

• Dance with your eyes shut and imagine you are on a shamanic journey to meet with your animal allies or your guides.

• Before you dance, consider a deity or archetype that you would like to embody. Do a prayer asking that energy fill you as you dance. Let the dance be an experience of that energy expressing itself through you.

Creative Writing for Personal Transformation

Through creative writing we can explore our personal experiences through our ability to express those experiences in the written word. That expression can create a sense of liberation. When what we feel and think move from an internalized sensation or experience into a manifest form, that energy is then liberated from the body energetic, freeing that emotion or energy, giving it means to fly.

There are many different types of writing. The majority of our experience with writing is merely the machination of the mind. Writing can conjure up more mind stuff. While that can be very interesting, it may not be all that useful towards the goal of spiritual development. When we focus our attention on conceptual reality, it can give the ego a stronghold to work from which can be contrary to spiritual liberation. In a spiritually liberated state, the ego becomes the horse instead of the driver of the cart. It is helpful to get the mind stuff out of the head and onto paper so that we are not running things over and over in our heads. We can get the old energetic baggage out of our bodies and give it a solid form through writing so we can say, "There it is, outside of me. I don't need it anymore. I can now release it." This can be a means to clearing the mind stream, which is extremely useful for personal transformation.

The type of writing that I am most interested in here is writing that integrates the conscious mind with the subconscious and superconscious minds. In this process, the writer allows the words to come through him freely instead of a more mental process in which he is using a lot of energy thinking things out. Not only does this sort of process potentially open up the writer to the deep wells of creativity beyond the standard mind stream, it can also help a writer move beyond writer's block. I believe writer's block is mainly a schism between the mind and the emotional body. Through writing techniques that connect us to the sub- and superconscious minds, we can bypass or transform these blockages and access this deeper creative fount.

One technique that is very helpful in accessing the different parts of the psyche is stream-of-consciousness writing. To do this, just place the pen on the page and begin to write without concern for sounding good or being coherent in any particular way without any editing. This can help you to get out of the linear mode within the creative process and allow deeper streams of possibility to come through. To access different streams of consciousness, you might find that it is helpful to tap into deeper aspects of yourself through meditation, movement or some other form of art, and then transpose that experience into the written word.

Exercise 2: Contacting the Subconscious Mind

The subconscious mind can be accessed by meditating on the sensations of the body. Spend a few minutes focusing in on the sensations and emotions held in the physical body. Pick up a pen and begin to write with your non-dominant hand (for example, if you are right handed, write with your left hand). People are accustomed to communicating the thoughts of the conscious mind through writing with the dominant hand. By writing with the non-dominant hand, it becomes easier to access the subconscious part of yourself. You can imagine that you are allowing an inner part of yourself to write with the hand. Allow the next letter to be a mystery, or listen to the mind stream accessed and then write it down with the non-dominant hand. Not only does this help you to access different parts of the self but it will also help you to release the notion of "getting it right," as speed, coherency and penmanship are likely to fall by the wayside.

Exercise 3: Poetry as an Expression of Spiritual Experience

When we have experiences of non-ordinary reality, we enter an altered state. The return from that state is very much like the return from dreaming to conscious awareness. Directly after the experience there is often still a sense of vividness. We are still between the worlds; we both remember what we experienced, *and* we are conscious of our waking reality. This state is an ideal time to practice prose and poetry as a way of integrating this altered state experience. When you do shamanic journeying, trance dance or some other kind of meditation, have a pen and paper nearby. In the process of returning to third-dimensional conscious, take out the paper and pen and allow that stream of consciousness to flow through you. Allow the stream to be expressed through the language of metaphor instead of purely a blow-by-blow description of the experience. You may find that this metaphoric language will more accurately express the way that you felt in that state rather than explaining it in linear descriptive terms.

Exercise 4: Automatic Writing

Through automatic writing, a person can receive communication from spiritual sources. This can be done with either the dominant or non-dominant hand. In automatic writing, a person allows a source of inspiration outside of himself or herself to direct the writing process.

First, begin by clearing the psychic space by smudging with sacred herbs and then surrounding yourself with white light.

• Invite your spiritual allies and guides to be present with you, lending their support and protection.

• Think of something that you would like to know, and imagine that you are asking these guiding and protecting spirits that question.

• Ask them to write through your hand.

• Place the pen to the paper and allow the answer to come through you. You may get a sense that your hand is being moved and the writing is coming through you, or you may hear the words in your head and the writing is like a form of transcription.

• Particularly in the beginning, concern yourself less with whether or not what you are receiving is correct. Concern yourself more with your ability to get out of the way and allow the wisdom through.

• After you are done, be sure to thank your guides. Clear the psychic space with smudge, and ground your energy by feeling your connection to the earth.

Image has Magic in It!

The word "image" is made up of the words "*I Mage*." All artists are magicians. Through the creation of visual art, we are performing magic with light. Without light, there is no vision. To be an artist, we are in relationship to light in all its spectrum of colors. We experience visceral responses to color. Looking at different colors can instantly change our mood and state of mind. Most of us have had the experience of trying to decide what color to wear on a given day. It is so woven into our experience that we forget the power that color has to influence how we feel. Through the use of color and light, we have the ability to effect change in our environment and ourselves. There is definitely a very special magic to this!

Visual art also uses the power of symbol to express archetypal themes. By creating and using symbols, we can influence the psyche. As we discussed before, symbol is the language of Spirit. We can use these symbols to help influence our psyche in positive directions for transformation. When we transpose these symbols onto a surface and then view them regularly, they become ingrained deeper and deeper within us, changing the river of consciousness from the subconscious on up. It is particularly powerful when a symbol is created with intention. Perhaps the symbol is one that arose in a dream or through a meditation. We might recognize the symbol as a common archetype such as those seen on tarot cards. No matter what the source, the symbol can help to direct both our conscious and unconscious minds towards an intention or state of being.

Throughout my house, I have pieces of art and sculpture that were created by myself or by others. They serve as markers or remembrances to help my psyche stay on course to remember the larger reality of the Divine. While I do not necessarily pay conscious attention to each of these objects over the course of a day, some part of me is still taking in their meaning and energy, and they affect the way that I think, the way that I feel, and the things that I do.

Exercise 5: How Does Art Affect You?

We are affected by the things that surround us. Most people's homes are a strong indicator of what we feel is important:

• Ask yourself "What is it that you would like to direct your energy towards in your life, particularly in relation to your spiritual inclinations?"

• Make a list of images or symbols that would symbolize those things for you.

• Notice what themes are present.

• Create or find some images that help you to focus in these ways and put them up in prominent locations so that you may help to direct your psyche towards those tendencies.

• You may find it interesting to walk around your house and ask yourself what the art in your house symbolizes to you.

Visual Art as the Expression of Essence

While some art is purely color and light-oriented, other art represents things in physical reality such as flowers, people, fruit, etc. To accurately represent an object, you must look not only at its color, shape and its relationship to light, but also at how one might convey the very essence of that object.

By meditating on and experiencing the essence of something, we can learn about its true nature. This act allows us to open ourselves to experience something beyond the self, expanding our consciousness beyond previous limitations.

When we attempt to express the essence of an object, we cannot help but also express our relationship to the object through the process. No two people will express essence in the same way because of this.

Exercise 6: Expressing Essence

• Find something you would like to draw, paint, or sculpt. It should be something that you can be in the same physical space with.

• Take time to experience it from all angles. Engage all of your senses in that experience. Notice how it makes you feel to look at it. Imagine what it would feel like to be that thing. Imagine that you become one with it.

• Now try to express the essence of that thing within your artistic process.

Sound and Spirit

Sound is vibration. Every sound that we hear is vibrating at a different frequency. When there are multiple sounds present, there is a relationship that happens between the vibrations. When those relationships of frequencies make us feel good, we tend to call it harmony, and when the relationship of those vibrations makes us feel uncomfortable, the frequencies are called dissonant.

Dissonance brings about chaos, and harmony creates order. Dissonance and chaos can shake us up to get us to make changes, and harmony creates peace and feelings of well-being, which help us to ascend to new levels of consciousness and health. On the whole, we want to harmonize the frequencies within ourselves and within others, though chaos and dissonance do have their place in our transformative process (in measured doses!) Most musicians seek to find ways to express sounds that are harmonically pleasing.

Frequencies can be described as the rhythm within the tone. When you pluck a guitar string, it vibrates back and forth at different speeds, depending upon the length and width of the string. Even a pure, clear, tone has a rhythm within it, and this rhythm is the frequency of the sound. You can have different tones being played simultaneously, but what is important is the relationship of one tone to the other. Certain tonal relationships create a harmonic resonance while other tonal relationships create a dissonant resonance.

All of our chakra centers and organs are vibrating at different frequencies. The frequencies of the different organs and chakras are like a beautiful symphony when they are vibrating harmonically. Harmonic resonances indicate a healthy body and psyche. When we have illness, there is a sustained dissonance occurring in the energetic field. Through the use of sound, we can assist the body energetic to come into a harmonic resonance between frequencies through the power of *entrainment.*

In 1665, Dutch scientist and inventor Christian Huygens began to develop the notion of entrainment. He found that when pendulum clocks were placed side by side on a wall, the swinging of the pendulums would eventually move into exact synchronized rhythm. When vibrations are in proximity, they tend towards synchronicity. [4] Through rhythmic entrainment within the body energetic, we can increase health and well- being by assisting the harmonic relationship in the body through music.

Listening to or playing music can increase our well-being on many levels. When we share music with others, we share the music itself as well as the vibration and energy that it engenders. We are creating a group resonant field with others that is the combination of the music, our relationship to the music, and our relationship to each other within the resonant field. There is a special magic that is created when people play music together. The music becomes a common media that can hold people together on many levels within its vibrational embrace.

In order to create entrainment within a group, profound listening is required. When participants are really listening, they can hear their place within the rhythmic fabric. The ego can have a place within this experience, but in order to really experience the group entrainment, the musicians must focus primarily on their relationship to the whole and less on the aggrandizement of the self. It is okay for the ego to have some fun though, and find pockets within the musical landscape to soar above and beyond and then to dive back down to submerge into the rhythmic or tonal entrainment. Drumming is a powerful example of this practice in action. When drumming or tone is sustained over time, people can easily access altered states that the rhythmic trance engenders. The rhythm creates a sonic container that allows the psyche to transport itself through the realms for healing and spiritual transformation.

Exercise 8: Entrainment

• Find a friend to do a tone experiment with you.

• Stand facing one another with your foreheads touching. Begin to make a clear sustained tone, such as "aaaaahhhh" or "eeeeee" in any pitch that feels comfortable for you.

• The other person should then join you and make the same sustained tone. You should do this for a few minutes.

• Play around and try to find a different pitch that harmonizes with the first pitch and sustain that for a little while.

• Now sit in silence for a time and notice how you feel.

Exercise 9: Rhythm and Entrainment

If you have a drum or a rattle, you can do a similar exercise with a friend. First, both of you play the same rhythm. Once you can hear that your beat is well synchronized, one of you can divide off and finds a rhythm that is different from the first. This new rhythm should meld and match with  the first rhythm and still be different. If you give it enough time, you can go beyond the mechanics of creating the rhythm and allow the rhythm to play you instead of you playing the rhythm. Many report that they feel as though their hands are being moved by some larger force when the mind is able to get out of the way.

The Art of Life

Art is not just painting, or music, dance or writing. Art is a way of approaching life. If you do not believe in your skills in any of the things we formally call art, it does not mean that you are not an artist. Art is the way that we interface our creativity with the actions of life. Art can be in the cooking of a meal. Art can be in the way we solve a problem or organize our homes. How can each of us make every day a work of art? I invite you to ponder and explore how art connects you to the essence of all your feelings and actions and expresses your own inner nature in all that you do. How does the inner artist work through you?

10

Attitude and Ethics

In Chapter 10, we come around full circle and begin a new octave of possibility. In numerology, multiple digit numbers are added together to reduce the sum down to a single digit number. In the case of ten, 1 and 0 are added together, bringing us back to the unity of one, but at a new level of understanding of our relationship to the Universe. Ten represents a new cycle. It is a journey into limitlessness based on our comprehension and integration of all that we have learned. With that knowledge, we are capable of rising to higher levels of consciousness and realize the highest of ideals that we might strive for. It is a rebirth in which we are able to build upon the lessons of the past so we might respond to life from a higher perspective. It represents self-mastery and recognition of how we fit into the sacred pattern of life.

Pythagoras believed that the number ten comprehended all arithmetic and harmonic proportions, containing all numbers, and therefore all things and possibilities. Ten represents a synergy, a whole that is greater than the sum of its parts.

In one, we focused on the principle of unity, and how all diversity is contained within that Unity. In ten, we will be examining the ways in which the self affects the whole. What are the ways in which we can be fully empowered as individuals in such a way that we honor the entirety? How can we align harmonically with the whole, while being true to ourselves?

Karmic Responsibility

Through focusing our intent and re-patterning our thoughts and emotions, we can alter both our internal and external realities. By owning and developing this ability, we can truly come into our power as the co-creators of our lives. This ability is not only a benefit but also a great responsibility. When we desire something that does not serve the greater whole, we ultimately hurt ourselves. Every action we take effects the whole of creation in some subtle manner. Since we are a part of the web of life, when we do something that hurts another person, it will return to us in some way. What we put out gets mirrored back to us. We are all connected. Together, we are one being. We cannot fulfill personal desires that hurt others with out hurting ourselves. When we realize that we are one with everything, it helps us to be aware of the consequences of our actions.

You cannot even move or breathe without affecting life around you. In 1963 mathematician and meteorologist Edward Lorenz coined the term "*The Butterfly Effect*." The premise behind the butterfly effect is that small changes in conditions could produce vast variations in the behaviors of a large system, such as the weather. For example, {perhaps} the flap of a butterfly's wing in Brazil could set off a tornado in Texas. [1]

There is no event or thing that is outside of the Divine Order. Even Chaos is a part of the larger schema. Chaos often is thought of as randomness and lack of order. Perhaps it is more accurate to think of it as events inside of a larger pattern than we can currently apprehend. That apparent randomness results from interactions within the larger *dynamical system*. Without being able to clearly see the larger picture, we lack the perspective that can show the Divine order of relationships between people, things, and events.

Ideally, we find a balance between control (free will) and release (non-attachment and trust), which helps us to be in balance between personal will and Divine will. Free will or personal will adds an element of chaos to the patterns of manifestation. That chaos can create explosive change. The Divine patterns held by the involutionary energies of the earth help to create order. There is synergy between chaos and order that makes for evolutionary change. The trick is for us to fully own and manifest our free will while harmonizing with Divine order. In this way we can bring about change without unnecessary destruction.

By focusing our intention to harmonize with Divine order, we a have a bit more of a chance to create positive change that keeps the whole in mind. Intention is a powerful tool for manifestation. By setting a strong intention, our connection to the Divine Mind can be more easily accessed so that we can bring about the fruition of our goals in a more harmonious way.

As our faith and ability to alter our reality grows, we develop more personal power. Because of this, it becomes even more important to be aware of the effect on the larger collective that our desires might have. With more power, you have the ability to exert a larger force upon collective reality. Therefore, when you want to draw some thing to yourself, you must take the whole into consideration.

Does what I want hurt or hinder any one else? Is this for my highest good, or does the desire and or creation of this thing somehow further entrench my negative patterns? Does it serve the highest good of all? These questions can help to clarify whether your personal inclination serves or detracts from the collective and your own highest good.

Honoring Interconnectedness

One way to honor the interconnectedness between all things is to set the intention that the benefits of your manifestation be bestowed on all beings. Not only do you receive the benefits of the setting of intent and the manifestation of that intent, you also help others, and receive good karma for assisting all of creation with your focused intent. When we identify ourselves as a part of the whole, instead of an entity separate from the whole, we become more in tune with the universal flow of energy and its blessings. The universe is infinite, and in that infiniteness, there is limitless potential.

Balancing Personal Desire and Non-Attachment

Sometimes what you really need will not come in the package you expected it in. It is a good idea to have very specific ideas about what you wish to create, but not to have specific expectations about what you will get. Expectations also imply attachment, and this too is a trap. Attachments can actually hinder your manifestation from occurring. Attachments imply that you already come from a place of lack, so you cannot manifest what you want because you are acting as if it is not yours already. Besides, with only a limited conscious knowledge of our soul's agenda, it is hard for us to determine what we truly need versus what we think we need.

Each of us came here with an agenda of personal transformation, both to complete unfinished karma as well as to expand our soul's experience and knowledge. Above and beyond our conscious desire for "success," we are here to learn and grow spiritually. The needs of the soul often are not synonymous with the needs of the ego. A balance between enlightened self interest and non-attachment puts us in a state in which we are more likely to be happy regardless of what appears to be going on.

Going for the True Goal

Most everything that we wish to manifest in the material world usually has less to do with the actual *thing* and more to do with the desire for the internal state of happiness and peace. A person might think: "I really want a fancy sports car." "I want to feel successful in my career." "I want a new house." But the reason that person might want those new things is in order to reach a desired state.

It is best to not be deluded into thinking that the means to the goal (house, car, job, wife) is the goal itself. It would serve us better to place our intention on the goal than on the means. The goal (happiness and peace) is attainable in every moment. We can get into a warped state of mind and forget what is really important. We get stubborn about our attachments to how we think reality is supposed to be showing up. Just by a change in our perception, we can have happiness, bliss, and peace because we chose it directly. In this way, it does not matter so much what is happening in the world. What matters is whether we are choosing the state internally. Applying the laws of manifestation, we have just as much power, if not more power, to change the internal state as the external state. It is a matter of choice.

Ultimately, the quest is not how we can alter reality, but how can we embrace reality in its entirety right now and honor the perfection in what is currently manifesting. There will always be one more mountain to climb, another goal to reach. We will never have everything we want. The best thing we can do is to release to and be content with the here and now. This is true freedom.

One of my teachers once told a story in which there was once a great king who told his court artists that he would give a great prize to the one that could really portray true peace in a painting. After a time, one of the artists brought to him a stunningly beautiful painting of a most peaceful lake up in the mountains that very few people had ever been to. Just by looking at the painting you could be lulled into a very peaceful state. A little while later, the other artist brought him a picture of a huge crashing waterfall, with water coming down in torrents. At the bottom of the waterfall was a small dove in a very peaceful state of meditation. The king gave this artist the prize. He said, "This painting reflects true peace. When you can be peaceful in the midst of chaos, this is peace in the truest sense. Anyone can be peaceful in a peaceful place." [3]

True Happiness
Comes from Within

True peace and happiness is a quality that comes from within. No amount of changing your external situation can change the way you feel. I once saw this very principle in action when traveling in India. We were in a beautiful stone carvers' village in South India called Mamallapuram. While walking along the road we stopped to look at some carvings that were for sale on the side of the road. Like most of the carvings in this town, the carvings were of Gods, Goddesses, Buddha, and other Divine beings and sacred symbols. Each was delicately carved and quite beautiful, each was infused with an inner beauty of spirit. The stone carver was a leper, dressed only in rags. Most of his fingers and toes were missing. He held the stone he was carving between his feet. He had a rags tied around his hands that he would slip a chisel into so he could chip away at the rock. The stone carver graciously greeted us, with love and peace shining out of every pore of his being. So great was his kindness that as we admired his carvings, He tried again and again to give away some of his precious wares to us.

There we were, middle class American foreigners in India. Our American dollars made us seem like jet setters compared to the native population. Here was this totally impoverished man who was a social pariah, so generously trying to give away his work. We bought a beautifully carved Buddha figure and a little Ganesh statue. He insisted on giving us a little pendant of stone with an Aum symbol carved in it. I left feeling that somehow we were the poor ones and he was the one with all the wealth. I have often wished I bought everything he had to sell, and yet I know he would have been just as happy without our money. I kept his carving of Buddha on my altar to remind myself that true riches come from within.

Burning Out Desire

Another way of looking at fulfillment of desires is from the left-hand tantra perspective, which promotes the fulfillment of desires as a means to releasing attachment to those desires. By experiencing the complete fulfillment of desires, the need for those desires to be fulfilled disappears.

On the other hand, the right-hand path of Tantra promotes the denial of desires in order to purify the system. I don't believe that there is one right way. Each person must find his or her own way in regards to this. It is all the Divine play in action. In Hinduism, the Divine play, called *Leela*, acknowledges that simultaneously, nothing matters and everything matters. The Divine is expanding itself and will continue to do so no matter what we decided to do or not do. Ultimately, we will evolve and transform regardless of whether we make the path long or short.

Our concern should not be success or failure but whether we are fully engaged in the opportunity to play in the game of life. The lesson is in the learning not in some concept of completion. Just as a universe goes on forever, so do we. Life is not a linear progression with a beginning and an end; it is a relational path that goes all directions and ends up in the same place.

Spiritual Ego and the Beginner's Mind

As you become more advanced spiritually, there is an ever present danger lurking called spiritual ego. "I'm so advanced!" "I know so much more about spirituality than those other people."

"Now I understand how it all works." Once we think that we have it all figured out, we lose the beginner's mind, which is essential for further growth. With the beginner's mind, we remain open to possibility and are less likely to limit our reality based on a concretized perception of how reality works. There are several tools that are helpful towards releasing spiritual ego, one of which is to embrace the paradox that there is no one right way. Reality is created by our filters, and there are at least as many filters as there are people. When we recognize that we cannot *figure out* reality with the mind, it helps us to focus on experience and sensation. A good motto to live by is, "Do not compare, do not judge. Release the need to know." These are all functions of the ego. The ego is meant to be a tool, not the one who operates the tool. As soon as the ego grasps onto spiritual development as a means for self-aggrandizement, our clear perception becomes warped. The ego's perceptions are not the same as the witness self's perceptions. The ego will always color the experience with its filter on reality. Pure witness-based perception is closer to a true merging with the Divine intelligence of the universe.

One tool that I use to keep my spiritual ego in check is the analogy of the tightrope. I am carefully walking along on a tightrope. To one side, I have the full awareness that I have access to all knowledge. I am able to perceive and work with energies that are present and have a glimpse of the grand designs of the universe. On the other side of the tightrope, I am still struggling deeply with my wrong perceptions, my negative beliefs and attitudes, and my negative emotions . I know I have a long way to go. Both things are true simultaneously. When I can be aware of both the fact that I am completely wrong and that I have full access to the Divine wisdom, it helps me to keep a clearer perspective. It keeps me humble while simultaneously supporting my belief in myself and my innate Divinity.

The Practice of Mindfulness

It is so important to get control of the mind so that the ego is not always dictating how we choose to respond to reality. By applying mindfulness, we constantly watch the motivations of the mind in order to purify our consciousness, thus make better choices that can bring us towards enlightenment. This requires an honest conversation with the self, in which we are always noticing the nature of the inner work that we need to focus on in order to bring us towards true inner peace and harmony. In particular, it is important to listen for the negative thoughts and emotions that cause discord and attempt to change that perception in order to make more positive choices. A lot of energy and head space is taken up by negative thoughts and emotions. We can re-channel that energy towards positive thoughts and goals.

There is power in the shadow self that can be mined and used well. Where there is fear, anger, shame, grief and guilt, there is power. When we set our attention and intention on transforming those emotions we can unlock that energy for positive use. The negative experiences that we have had have served a purpose. Our hardships are the refiner's fire that ultimately tempers the steel of our souls, making us stronger and more resilient. It takes a lot of pressure to make a diamond out of coal. Similarly, to awaken the enlightened self we often must experience hardship in order to gain knowledge. We learn not only from our positive experiences but from our negative ones as well. The trick is not to allow ourselves to perpetuate negative beliefs as a result of challenging experiences.

The Power of Your Word and the Importance of Integrity

When you stalk power, power stalks you. The more you hone your attention and intention, and the more developed you become, the quicker things can manifest in your life, both positive and negative. This is another reason that it is essential to approach life from a strong position of integrity simultaneous to the development of power, ability and knowledge.

I cannot stress enough how important the power of your word is. Your word is your truth. Only commit to that which you mean to follow through on.

When you make empty assertions and don't follow through, your word becomes meaningless. The word and the will are inextricably linked. When you mean what you say and you say what you mean, your word gains power. If you cannot follow through when you give your word, it is important to attempt to be accountable at the very least.

Don't say "Yes" when you mean "No." When your word is not expressing your will, but instead expresses an unconscious need to placate without a desire to follow through, it is a manifestation of how you are split internally. When you are split internally, you halve your available power. When you speak your truth with sincerity and then follow through with clarity, you express your integrity.

The Fastest Path to Enlightenment

A friend of mine once asked Indian Saint Ananda Moy Ma, "What is the fastest path to enlightenment?" She replied, "Always tell the truth."

When we speak and live our truth, it aligns us with not only that which we feel good about, it also keeps us conscious of where we might be missing the mark. Instead of investing in our ego's need to always be right, we have the opportunity to acknowledge where we still have work to do and that can help to keep us on track with our spiritual growth.

When we see what we need to work on, we can view those frailties from a perspective of discernment instead of judgment. From this viewpoint, we see what can change within us with a sense of humor and an attitude of loving kindness. By seeing ourselves with clarity and compassion, we are truly free to grow and expand because we are not changing as a result of fear, punishment or loss of love. We are changing because we choose to see the truth from a compassionate perspective.

What Are You Doing to Make a Difference in the World?

We are beings with free will figuring out how to individuate while being inextricably interlinked with all that is. It is a conundrum of infinite proportions. How do we express our individuality while honoring the wholeness of All that Is?

A big part of answer to that question is to figure out what you want to offer the world, and get to it. How can you express the essence of your passion *and* create positive change? Individuation and interdependence do not have to be at odds with one another.

So many people are unhappy because they are spending their lives in jobs that do not fulfill them. They allow themselves to be cornered into forty hours of misery a week due to fear regarding survival, fear of loss of approval or a lack of motivation and direction. Self-limiting beliefs keep people living small. I believe we are here to live to the fullest of our potential and have the potential create the best reality possible.

Don't let your beliefs limit you! What is your secret dream for yourself? What excuses are you making to not fulfill that dream? Is that wish truly unfulfillable (e.g. I wish I had wings) or are you letting your limitation win?

Re-awakening inner passion can open the way to a more fulfilling life based on both creativity and positive purpose. Those inner passions and dreams are the bread crumb trail that will help you to answer that age old question, "Why am I here?" I believe everyone has a sacred purpose here on this Earth, whether it is to be a doctor, an artist, a gardener, a scientist, or a house cleaner. Even the lowliest job has nobility if it is done with dedication and positive intent. Every day, we can be the ones who change the world for the better, even if our livelihood is not the primary way in which we do that. Leave flowers where you walk.

Wherever you go or whatever you do, how can you create more beauty, more joy, more peace or more harmony? If everyone were looking to do this, the world would definitely be a better place for everyone.

The Profound Power of Loving Kindness

One of the most powerfully transformative outlooks that we can view reality from is the lens of compassionate awareness. When we practice loving kindness towards ourselves and others, something really miraculous occurs. When that love is truly allowed in and integrated, the ego's defensive posture can drop away. What remains when that façade is left behind is the pure shining essence of the soul without pretense. That love can set each of us free to be our illuminated self without the self-mortification that limits our potential as human beings.

Most people intuitively know how healing love can be. Many people dream of truly being in love. Unfortunately, romantic love is rarely completely unconditional, and that unconditional love is what most people deeply crave. It is the greatest healer of all. The person best suited to give you that kind of love is yourself. It's really a good idea to cultivate that self-love, as you have to live with yourself no matter what. There is no getting away or leaving. It is much better to resign yourself to unconditionally loving yourself than to conditionally loathing yourself.

Self Love

Self love is so important for personal transformation. Self love is not selfish. It is the ultimate self-care. You can care for yourself above and beyond what another person can possibly do for you. When you fall in love with yourself, you cultivate a state of internal love that shines out into the world. When you love

yourself, you have more love to give. Your attitude towards yourself affects your ability to love and be loved by others. If you hate yourself, it will make it more difficult for you to manifest loving relationships. Love is a much more preferable state. Not only does it feel good, it actually creates more positive energy within and around you.

Negative energy, emotions and thoughts can suck energy from a space. Have you been with someone who was in a negative emotional state and then noticed that you felt depleted afterwards? Conversely, people that emanate loving kindness emanate a positive energy that directly affects the people and the environment around them. Buddhists call the practice of emanating of loving kindness *Metta*. The cultivation of self-love can help you to be happy no matter what is going on, and it can make others happy too.

Sometimes people find it easier to love others than to love themselves. After so much conditioning that says we are not supposed to love ourselves, it is no surprise. The problem lies in the belief that somehow love will puff up the ego. Perhaps with a slight perspective shift, we can focus the lens of our love on that pure blessed child within each of us that truly needs and deserves our love in order to be whole. With this realization, the taboo of self-love can be dissolved.

When you really love yourself, you love yourself warts and all, not only the part of you that you think deserves love. It means loving the whole package. That's what unconditional love is. It is the get down and roll around in the mud loving with full acceptance. That love understands there will be change and growth. Tomorrow, you'll be in a new place. Today, you are where you are. Real unconditional love is accepting yourself and/or others without reservation.

If an individual was not raised with loving kindness, sometimes that person might need to learn how to love and be loved by someone who knows how to express loving kindness. Ideally, we might like to believe that ability to show love is inherent. After years of working with many people, it has become apparent to me that the expression love and loving touch are learned behaviors. Luckily, many people have an aunt, a grandparent or a family friend that they learned a bit about loving and being loved from, even if their parents did not know how to express love. This is a huge asset. From the seed of that loving relationship can grow the attitude and experience of loving kindness. Ultimately, the love of others can help us to love ourselves so that deep soul healing can occur.

> We can live without religion and meditation, but
> we cannot survive without human affection. [4]
> — His Holiness the Dalai Lama

All negative emotions relate back to our relationship with love. Grief is the sadness of loss of love. Anger is the emotion a person feels when that person believes he or she is not loved or appreciated. Fear is fear of loss of love or life. Shame is fear of loss of love due to prior thoughts or deeds. It almost always comes back to our great need for love, kindness and appreciation.

A part of the way we learn to be loving is by watching how unloving we really are. When we get angry, scared, or distant, when the internal judge comes out and pronounces a judgment; we can clearly see how we are making distance to somehow avoid anything that appears to be "not-love." Truly choosing to be unconditionally loving means making a unilateral decision to love in the face of whatever is being presented. It means loving no matter what appears to be going on. It's no easy task to love even when those around us may not be making that choice. Love is an internal state. We can be loving when things are going well. We can be loving when we are making boundaries, when we are creating endings, and when we are standing up for ourselves. Love does not have to mean giving up sovereignty in any way. It means we can love and be loved even if we might disagree. When we can drop the confusion and separate the need for love from the need for power, we are more likely to get both.

The people who appear to be our enemies are in fact, our best friends. They create a perfect opportunity to develop the powerful characteristics of patience, strength and compassion. It's easy to be loving and compassionate with others when they are being loving and kind back to us. Difficult situations and people can get us to look at where we might develop a greater ability to be in our truth despite differences. Those people or situations might force us to love ourselves no matter what anyone else thinks. They can help us to see where we might be missing the mark. They could also show us where we might develop greater tolerance and acceptance.

Our enemies get us to do the things we try to avoid doing. It makes us grow in the ways we really need to grow, not just the ways we think we'd like to grow. In this way, our enemies are our real friends, because they help us to grow more than anyone else. These beings offer us one of our best shots at enlightenment. They deserve our love.

When we are feeling loving, we experience a greater sense of peace, and that peace affects everything and everyone around us. Love in its many forms is a great unifier. Love dissolves the veils of isolation and separation, allowing each of us to become more fully ourselves. One of the greatest contributions we can make to the world is to foster more loving kindness by being the change we want to see. Love is the great harmonizer, and the ultimate healer. Love is the glue that holds the universe together. By cultivating loving kindness, we participate in the healing of ourselves, those around us, the rifts between cultures, classes, religions and species. Loving kindness is our greatest hope for harmonious survival. Through love we can learn to listen and share. It can help us to be spacious yet caring. We can feel supported so each can learn to stand strong. Through love, there is room both to change and grow and to feel woven with all that is.

Loving Kindness Meditation

Place your hands on the heart. Feel your own love for yourself. Remember all those who have loved you. Feel the sensation of that love that still lives there. Remember also, all those you have loved, feel the sensation of that love in your heart. Think now on all the things you love... a beautiful sunset, a piece of music, or favored activities. Feel that as sensation as well. Pets are a great source of unconditional love. If you have or have had a beloved pet or pets, feel the love they gave you and feel your love for these precious ones.

When you inhale, breathe in the love from all of these beings, and when you exhale, imagine your love pouring out of your heart to the world. When you inhale, feel the cosmos loving you. When you exhale, feel your love for all that is. Continue like this for a time.

Imagine you have a radiant smile in your heart. You can make a smile on your face and then transfer that sensation to your heart. Feel your heart shining with love. Feel the healing power of love within and around you. You are love.

May you feel completely loved. May you love completely.

Om Lokah Samastah Sukhino Bhavantu
Shanti, Shanti, Shanti
May all beings be happy.
May all beings be at peace.

Endnotes

Introduction

1. Marianne Williamson, *Illuminata: A Return to Prayer* (1995)

2. Gautama Buddha, from *The Dhammapada*

3. Gautama Buddha, source unknown

Chapter 1

1. From S.C. Malik, *Matter is Consciousness* from the book *The Nature of Matter,* vol. 4, ed. Jayant V. Narlikar (1995), an author's note on the semantic use of the word *Universe* as used in this book: "The Universe is everything that is and ever has or will be; there can be only one. To speak of many universes is therefore misuse of the term. If there could be many, they must somehow, in some sense, be mutually related; otherwise they could not be distinguished, or counted, or regarded as a many. They must constitute a single complex, within which there may be many distinguishable regions or epochs, but these would not be strictly be Universes, even if between them no communication of information could pass. If they exist they must have some kind

of togetherness. So long as they can be at all conceived and postulated, they will all form part of the all-inclusive Universe."

2. Mevlana Jelaluddin Rumi, excerpted from the prose pieces "The Indian Tree" and "One Song" from *The Soul of Rumi,* ed. Coleman Barks (2002)

3. His Holiness the Dalai Lama, *How to Expand Loving Relationships* (2005)

4. Author's note: While there is much to be learned from the spiritual systems of other cultures, it is also a very touchy subject. Cultural appropriation can water down and alter traditional teachings, as well as cause some very hard feelings for those people who are sensitive to these issues. Many feel an instinctual connection to the Earth, and non-ordinary reality, but the spiritual systems they were raised in did not give them teachings and ceremonies to make the proper connections. How can we weave cultural wisdoms and not step on toes? I don't have the answer to this, but it is a point of inquiry that we should all consider carefully.

5. From an interview with Michio Kaku by Stephen Marshall, Guerrilla News Network, The Prophets Conference, New York City, May 2001

6. References to morphic fields from the Rupert Sheldrake Online website: http://www.sheldrake.org/papers/Morphic/morphic_intro.html

Chapter 2

1. Ronald Goldman, *Circumcision, The Hidden Trauma: How an American Cultural Practice Affects Infants and Ultimately Us All* (1997)

2. Statistics from the U.S. Department of Justice 2004 National Crime Victimization Survey

3. Marilyn Ferguson, *The Aquarian Conspiracy: Personal and Social Transformation in Our Time* (1986)

4. Harville Hendrix, *Getting the Love You Want: A Guide for Couples* (1988)

5. Swami Satyasangananda, Tattwa Shuddhi (2003), pg. 6
Chapter 3
1. Enid Hoffman, *Huna: A Beginner's Guide* (1976)

2. Serge Kahili King, source unknown.

3. MacHaelle Small Wright, *Behaving as if the God in All Life Mattered* (1997). Author's note: Sri Aurobindo considered involution to be the path in which a spirit comes into a material form. Conversely, evolution could be thought of as the spiritualization of the material world. From this perspective, one might infer that matter is the reason why our spirit has become unconscious. From my perspective, the earthly realm has more potential to be heavenly if we could wake up and actualize that potential through the spiritualization of our emotions, thoughts and actions. The Divine realm could be realized while in body if we could find a perfect balance between harmony with the natural patterns, and the spiritualization of the psyche.

Chapter 5
1. Author's note: Today's physicists have rejected the notion of ether. However, the notion of an organizing principle and the existence of a medium for transformation makes sense to me. I'm holding out for the possibility that a working theorem for what ether is has not been tested properly or proven as of yet.

2. Swami Satyasangananda, *Tattwa Shuddhi* (2003)

3. Fred A. Wolf, *Taking the Quantum Leap: The New Physics for Nonscientists* (1989), pg. 60

Chapter 6
1. Elizabeth Webber and Mike Feinsilber, *Merriam-Webster's Dictionary of Allusions* (1999)

2. Gautama Buddha, from *The Dhammapada,* verse 2

3. His Holiness the Dalai Lama, *How to Expand Loving Relationships* (2005)

4. Author's note: There are differing notions about the proper location of the assemblage point. My understanding is that there

are three types of assemblage points and each has a different function. The heart center unifies the perception of the self as Divine without ego illusions.

5. You can find out more about Cheyenne Maloney's philosophy regarding the assemblage point and assemblage point shift at http://www.assemblagepointshift.com

Chapter 7
1. C. G. Jung, *The Archetypes and The Collective Unconscious (Collected Works)*
2. Dream catcher info can be found at http://www.native-languages.org/dreamcatchers.htm
3. C. G. Jung, *The Archetypes and The Collective Unconscious (Collected Works)*
4. Stephen La Barge and Howard Rhinegold, *Exploring the World of Lucid Dreaming* (1990), pg. 107
5. Namkhai Norbu, *Dream Yoga and The Practice of Natural Light* (1992), pp.50-51
6. Stephen La Barge and Howard Rhinegold, *Exploring the World of Lucid Dreaming* (1990), pg. 104

Chapter 9
1. Introduction by Gail Thomas, *The Muses* (1994)
2. See http://www.amc-music.com/drumstudy
3. Herbert Benson, *The Relaxation Response* (1976)
4. See http://en.wikipedia.org

Chapter 10
1. James Gleick, *Chaos: Making a New Science* (1988)
2. See http://www.spiritual-teachers.com/stories/zen.htm
3. Mata Amritananda Mayi, from a discourse given in Los Angeles, June 2004.
His Holiness the Dalai Lama, source unknown

Biographies

Sylvia Brallier is the Director of The Tantric Shamanism Institute in Las Vegas, NV. She is a Master Hypno-therapist, Kriya Tantra Yoga instructor, Reiki Master, and Empathic Healer. She has been teaching healing and tantric shamanism workshops internationally since 1988. Her work is based on her own experiences with both ancient and new techniques for the evolution of consciousness.

Kiva Singh already knew she aspired to be an artist at the age of four. Through the nurturing environment of home schooling she was allowed the freedom to develop her art work. This is her first published collaboration with her mother, Sylvia. Along side her illus-tration, Kiva is currently working as model. She is focusing on her paintings, and looks forward to illustrating more literature in the future.

Illustrations

Illustrations by Kiva Singh can be found on the following pages:

6, 9, 11, 12, 20, 23, 24, 26, 36, 39, 42, 55, 56, 58, 64, 78, 84, 88, 98, 102, 103, 104, 110, 123, 130, 133, 136, 138B, 140, 142, 148, 154, 160, 161, 162, 164, 167, 174, 182, 188

Illustrations by Sylvia Brallier can be found on the following pages:

14, 22, 40, 43, 53, 57, 59, 68, 69, 70, 71, 77, 80, 87, 95, 112, 114, 120, 128, 138A, 149, 150, 151, 152, 153, 166, 175, 177, 179, 184, 185, 187, 194, 200, 204

Glossary

Aboriginal: The indigenous cultures throughout the world that are the original known inhabitants of an area..

Aborigines: Indigenous Australians.

Affirmation: A positive statement that may be used to help transform consciousness, and thus transform what is manifesting within a person's life.

Ajna chakra: Chakra between the brows that relates to spiritual vision and expanded perception. Also known as the third eye.

Akasha: Sanskrit for ether.

Akashic records: Akashic records are the cosmic record of everything that has ever been and ever will be.

Alchemy: The process of transforming literal or figurative lead into gold.

Alpha male: male that is either physically, psychologically, or socially in a position of power within a group.

Anahata: Chakra relating to the heart and connection located in the center of the chest.

Androgyny: Possessing both masculine and feminine traits.

Anima: The male part of the psyche.

Animal Ally: Supernatural animistic-based relationship between a human and the essential energy of animal species which can provide magical assistance to the shamanic practitioner.

Animus: The female part of the psyche.

Archetypes: Symbols that exist within the collective unconsciousness that are blueprints that represent different ways of being.

Assemblage Point: The bio-energetic center of the mode of perception within the field of an individual.

Astral Parasites: Astral creatures who feed on the energy of others. The majority of which have little or no consciousness beyond the compulsion to feed.

Astral travel: The conscious mind/astral body traveling through ordinary or non-ordinary reality without the restrictions of the body.

Athame: ceremonial knife used to delineate sacred space.

Aumakua: The high self in the Kahuna system of magic.

Auric Field: The energy field around the body.

Bindu: Sanskrit, referring to a focal point at the posterior fontanel of the head.

Brahma: Hindu God of creation. Consort of Saraswati.

Butterfly Effect: Small variations in the initial conditions of a dynamical system produce large variations in the long term behavior of the system.

Caduceus: Magic wand of the Greek God Hermes messenger of the gods. Also said to represent the three major channels of energy in the spine.

Carl Jung: pioneer in the field of human psychology

Causal Realm: the realm of pure formless consciousness that is prior to the emergence of form or manifestation.

Cellular Memory: An interaction of thought and emotion that creates an ingrained repeated effect on the biochemistry of a physical organism.

Censer: Vessel used for the burning of incense.

Centering: The process of returning focus to the internal self, creating a sense of stability, balance and individuation.

Chakra: Energy vortexes in the body which focalize and express different aspects of the psyche.

Chalice: Ceremonial vessel representing the water element and its attendant attributes.

Chi: Vital life force energy also known as prana and mana.

Clairaudience: Intuitive ability expressed through the sense of hearing.

Collective Unconscious: A term coined by Carl Jung referring to the part of a person's unconscious which is connected to all human beings through the morphic field. Archetypes exist with in the collective consciousness represented by the common symbols held by all people, e.g. "the Great Mother."

Consensual Reality: Reality as perceived and created by the consciousness of the collective.

Cosmic Map: A blueprint for the harmonious functioning of all the interrelated parts and aspects of planetary existence.

Cosmology: Theoretical model which describes a person's world view that can include non-physical energies and beings that influence reality.

Creating the Container: The process of defining and maintaining the psychic boundaries between the mundane and mystical realities.

Dalai Lama: Spiritual leader of the Tibetan people.

Demeter: Greek mother goddess of agriculture who represents ripeness, fertility, fulfillment, stability, and power.

Devas: the over lighting spirits of nature.

Devocation: Releasement of energies that have been called in for a particular purpose in a ceremony.

Dharma: The natural flow of the universal energy in alignment with Divine Law

Dissonance: In music, it is an interval or chord in which the tones oscillate in an inharmonious rhythmical relationship.

Divination: The process of discerning possible reality manifestation anywhere on the time line by psychical means.

Dogma / Dogmatic: Rigid spiritual doctrine which is authoritarian in nature and not to be questioned or doubted.

Double Helix: Two congruent twisted shapes (like a spring, screw or a spiral staircase) with a similar axis. DNA is a double helix.

Double Orobouros: Symbol of two serpents swallowing each other that signifies volatility and/or the balance of our upper and lower natures

Double Standard: A rule which is applied more stringently to one party than to others, particularly relating to the stricter moral behavior demanded of women than of men.

Dr. Harville Hendrix: Co-author, Getting the Love You Want and originator of Imago match relationship therapy..

Dream Catcher: A Native American spiritual tool. A web with a hole in the center built on a hoop, whose purpose is to "capture" good dreams and allow the bad dreams/ energies to pass through the hole.

Dreamtime: This term is commonly used by the aboriginal peoples of Australia to describe non-linear reality.

Duality: The premise that everything has an opposing force

Dynamical System: Mathematical concept in which a fixed rule describes the time dependence of a point in geometrical space.

Edward Lorenz: American mathematician, meteorologist, a contributor to the chaos theory and inventor of the strange attractor notion. He coined the term butterfly effect.

Ego: The part of the psyche that perceives of all reality as separate and distinct from itself and primarily invested in individuation and self justification.

Electrostatic Forces: Forces exerted by a static (i.e. unchanging) electric field upon charged objects.

Elementals: Air fire, water, earth and ether. Also can be used to describe the non-corporeal entities which are associated with the elements.

Endorphins: Peptides produced by the pituitary gland and the hypothalamus that resemble opiates in their ability to produce analgesia and a sense of well-being that can act as natural pain killers.

Enlightened Masters: People who have achieved a very high level of spiritual awareness who are dedicated to making positive change by helping others.

Enlightenment: The process or state of embodying the Divine.

Entrainment: Principle of physics in which two or more oscillating bodies in proximity tend to synchronize rhythmically.

Esoteric: Knowledge of an inner nature that is secret or not generally known.

Ether: A unifying force field

Evolutionary Energies: Entities and energies that assist in the transformative process of evolution that can create physical, mental, emotional an spiritual change beyond what has been previously known.

Externalizing: Blaming outside forces for occurrences rather than believing that all reality is ultimately created subjectively.

Fetishes: A small carving that represents an animal ally that is carried or placed on an altar to empower to connection with a specific animistic force.

Fight or Flight Response Mechanism: Animal instinctual response when faced with danger to either face the threat ("fight"), or avoid the threat ("flight").

Fire Walking: A ceremony where participants on hot coals without getting burned after performing a special ritual of preparation.

Fractal Pattern: A visual representation of a mathematical equation which continues to multiply and expand based on a root pattern.

Ganesh: Elephant headed Hindu deity, son of Parvati and Shiva, who is said to remove obstacles and oversees new beginnings.

Generative Force: Productive creative energy

Gnomes: Elemental spirits of Earth.

Golden Shadow: The Golden Shadow is our own disowned potential that we project onto others that we admire who appear to possess characteristics we believe are beyond our capacity.

Hara: The center of a person's gravity, awareness, energy, and activity located below the navel.

Hatha: Sanskrit. 'Ha' means sun and 'tha' means moon. Can also mean force. System of yoga that aims to create a state of equilibrium through balancing various forces.

Hecate: Greek crone goddess keeper of the crossroads, who is wise with of a lifetime of experience.

Holographic Perception: The ability to create a new level of perception of reality through merging varied perspectives

Hypnotherapy: A form of therapy in which the therapist induces altered state of consciousness in the client, characterized by heightened suggestibility and receptivity to direction in order to make positive changes in behaviors, emotions, thought patterns or relationship to sensations.

Ida: Sanskrit. The feminine or moon channel of energy which spirals up the spine beginning and ending on the left side of the body.

Imago: Description of a type or relationship in which a person unconsciously chooses a partner who exhibits characteristics similar to one's parents or siblings. This type of relationship often brings up unresolved psychological material to resolve.

Initiates: An Initiate is someone who has formally or informally dedicated themselves to a spiritual path or discipline.

Integrity: Remaining whole or undivided, creating a state of completeness by adhering to one's personal ethical and moral code.

Interconnectivity: The ability to be mutually connected.

Involutionary: Energies that are inherent in the earth.

Jackson Pollock: Abstract expressionist painter most famous for his works from the 1940's and 50's.

Kaala: Ray or force that emanates from bindu.

Kahuna: The Hawaiian system of magic and healing. A high level practitioner of Huna Magic, or any authority such as a professor.

Kali: A fierce Hindu Tantric Goddess who assists in the release of attachment and ego. Kali is the goddess of time and of transformation.

Karma: The metaphysical principle of cause and effect as it relates to the direction of our thoughts and actions .

Kaula Tantric practitioner: Red or left handed path of tantra in which the practitioner moves beyond attractions and repulsions in order to reach enlightenment instead of avoiding the push and pull of attraction and repulsion.

Kore: Greek maiden Goddess (also known as Persephone) who is pure and expansive representing new beginnings.

Kundalini: The serpent energy of the Goddess which rises up the spine bringing about enlightenment.

Lakshmi: Hindu Goddess of abundance, consort of Vishnu

Leela: Hindu belief that phenomenal reality is merely the play of the Gods, and does not tangibly exist.

Left-handed tantra: Tantric practitioners who break certain taboos after much purification to move towards enlightenment instead of choosing the path of abstinence.

Liminal: Identity dissolution. A state of undetermined orientation in which a new perspective may be found

Lucid Dreaming: The ability to be conscious while dreaming and physically sleeping.

Macrocosmic: Large, versus microcosmic, small. According to the golden mean, the pattern of the small can be found in the large and visa versa.

Mamallapuram: A 7th century port city of the South Indian dynasty of the Pallavas around 60 km south from the city of Chennai in Tamil Nadu, India. (Also known as Mahabalipuram)

Mana: Life force energy, also know as chi, or vital force

Manipura: Chakra center located in the solar plexus that relates to the power of will.

Mata Amritananda Mayi: Saint from Kerala India, known for her loving compassion and tireless service to humanity.

Metaphysical: Philosophical inquiry into conceptions of reality, including ontology, and the philosophies of religion, mind and perception.

Metta: The Buddhist practice of emanating loving kindness.

Microcosmic: Small (see macrocosmic.)

Middle World: Non-ordinary version of third-dimensional reality.

Moebius strip: A Moebius strip is a one-edged geometric surface with only one continuous side, formed by giving a 180 degree twist to a narrow, rectangular strip of paper and then connecting the two ends together.

Morphic Fields: Fields of energy or awareness which appear to influence behavior and/or biology

Muladhara: The first chakra center located near the perineum that relates to survival issues.

Nada: Sanskrit. Vibration

Nadi or Nadis: Energy channels in the body according to Vedic philosophy. Similar to Taoist version of the energy channels, often called meridians.

Nadi Shodhana: Tantric exercise that balances the male and female energy channels going up the spine, and the hemispheres of the brain.

Nagual Reality: Non-ordinary reality

Natural Law: Fundamental principles derived from the natural world that are not the creation of human societies or governments.

Newton, Sir Issac: English physicist, mathematician, astronomer, alchemist, inventor and natural philosopher who created the theory for universal gravitation and the three laws of motion, laying the groundwork for classical mechanics.

Niels Bohr: Danish physicist who made essential contributions to understanding atomic structure and quantum mechanics.

Non-ordinary Reality: Reality as perceived from a multidimensional perspective

Orisha: An aspect or Spirit of the Divine in lineages stemming from Yoruba, including Imago, Oyotunji, Candomblé and Lucumí/Santería.

Orobouros: Mythic serpent who swallows its own tail as an archetypal symbol of regeneration.

Out of Body: also know as astral travel. The process whereby a person's consciousness leaves the physical vehicle of the body.

Over-lighting Spirit: See Wraith Energy

Paradigm: A belief system.

Paradox: Two differing or opposing truths that are perceived as true simultaneously.

Parashakti: Hindu Goddess. The supreme energy.

Patriarchal: A societal construct in which men possess greater power in relationship to influence, money and privilege than women.

Personas: Inner characters.

Pingala: The male or sun channel of energy that spirals the spine beginning and ending on the right side of the body.

Polarity: Two opposing forces which are complementary in nature.

Polyamory: A type of love relationship in which a person may be in relationship with more than one person simultaneously.

Positionality: A strong belief in the correctness of subjective reality.

Power Loss: A shamanic term describing a condition in which a person has lost power due to trauma, and/or negative projections about the nature of reality.

Prana: Life force energy, also know as chi, vital force, or mana

Psycho pomp: A person who talk with, and potentially helps the dead to communicate to the living or to transmigrate to higher realms.

Pythagoras: Pythagoras made influential contributions to philosophy and religious teaching in the late 6th century BC in Greece. He believed that everything was related to mathematics, and thought that everything could be predicted and measured in rhythmic patterns or cycles.

Quantum physics: Quantum physics provides accurate and precise descriptions for many phenomena including the behavior of systems based on the atomic and subatomic level.

Quintessence: The Alchemists name for the fifth element, or ether.

Ritual: A repeated ceremony that reinforces sacred intent and the energy to support that intent by the placing of attention.

Rupert Sheldrake: British biologist who developed a hypothesis of morphogenetic fields, and has researched animal and plant development and behavior, telepathy, perception and metaphysics.

Sacred Space: A space and time made sacred by the setting of intention and the placing of attention for the purpose of celebrating or transforming reality magically.

Sahasrara: Chakra located at the crown of the head that relates to the process of enlightenment.

Saint Ananda Moy Ma: "The Joy-filled Mother." Indian spiritual master who came into this life fully realized.

Salamanders: Spirits of fire.

Sami Shaman Ailu Gaup: The Sami are an indigenous people who form an ethnic minority in Norway, Sweden and Finland. Ailu hails from Lapland.

Sandhya: Sanskrit. Union or joined. The perfect balance of the polarities within an individual. Also describes the place between sleeping and waking.

Sanghyang: Balinese ritual trance dance.

Sanskrit: Ancient language of the Aryan people, who migrated to India from Europe some time between 6000BC-1200BC.

Saraswati: Hindu Goddess of knowledge, music and all the creative arts. Consort of Brahma.

Serge Kahili King: Author, humanitarian and curator of the Hawaiian Art Museum on Kauai.

Shakti: Hindu Tantric Goddess who is an embodiment of the primal energy, who is formless. Consort of Shiva.

Shakti-Shiva energy: The dynamic relationship between energy filled emptiness and awakened awareness.

Shamanic / Shamanism: A body of practices in which the practitioner's consciousness travels between ordinary and non-ordinary reality to access information and healing for self and / or others.

Shiva: Hindu Tantric deity who is the embodiment of awakened awareness, and the destroyer of illusion. Consort of Shakti/Kali.

Shushumna: The central channel of energy that travels up the center of the spine

Simultaneous Time: A hypothesis that in other dimensional realities beyond the third there is no perception of past or future. All events are occurring simultaneously in an ever present now.

Smudging: Cleansing the energy field of a person, place or thing with sacred herbs or resins.

Soul Fragment: A aspect of a person's consciousness which has split into another dimension in order to avoid pain and trauma.

Soul Retrieval: A therapeutic process in which a soul fragment is recovered and reintegrated through shamanic means.

Spirit: An entity in any level or dimension of existence with some level of consciousness.

Spirit Guides: Entities who are committed to watch out for the well being of an individual for the entirety of that individual's life.

Star Beings: Refers to entities whose origins are extraterrestrial.

Star Tetrahedron: three dimensional form, it becomes two interpenetrating pyramids

Strong Nuclear Forces: One of the four fundamental forces of nature. The force between two or more nucleons, affecting the binding of nucleons into nuclei and the scattering of two nucleons.

Swadhisthana: A chakra located below the navel that relates to sexuality and vitality.

Sylphs: Elemental spirits of Air.

Symbology: The study, use or interpretation of symbols or symbolism

Syncretistic Philosophy: An attempt to reconcile disparate, even opposing, beliefs and to meld practices of various schools of thought.

Synthesis: Integration of ideas or energies. Combining of separate elements to form a coherent whole.

T'ai Chi Tu: Also known as the yin/yang symbol, which represents the dynamic balance between the active a receptive polarities.

Talmud: An authoritative record of rabbinic discussions on Jewish law, Jewish ethics, customs, legends and stories.

Tanoti: Sanskrit. Expansion

Tantra: "Tan" means to expand or weave, and "tra" means liberation. A vast body of related spiritual lineages that seek spiritual liberation through the remembrance of their Divine nature through inner balance, and recognition of the Divine in all things..

Taoist: An approach to life which seeks to honor and align with the universal principle as inherent in nature through taking proper action in its proper time and place, honoring an individuals capabilities and limitations.

Telepathy: Mind to mind comprehension or communication.

Theta brain wave state: A state of deep relaxation and meditation, enhanced creativity, stress relief, light sleep and dreaming, corresponding to brain frequencies ranging from 4Hz to 8 Hz.

Toltec: A path of nagualism, in which awareness, transformation, and intent are primary considerations.

Tonal Reality: Linear, ordinary reality.

Transpersonal Psychology: A school of psychology that studies the transcendent, or spiritual dimensions of humanity. Includes the study of human potential, and seeks the realization of unitive, spiritual, and transcendent states of consciousness.

Trayati: Sanskrit. Liberation

Triquetra: Three sided symbol used to represent the triune nature of the Divine.

Tungus: Siberian ethnic group, numbering perhaps 30,000, who live in the area from the Yenisei and Ob river basins to the Pacific Ocean and from the Amur River to the Arctic Ocean, and on the coast of the Okhotsk Sea.

Uhane: The conscious mind or self according to the Huna system of healing and magic.

Undines: Elemental spirits of water.

Unified Field Theory: A theory, if proven, that could tie together all known phenomena to explain the nature and behavior of all matter and energy in existence.

Unihipili: The subconscious mind or self according to the Huna system of healing and magic.

Vishnu: Hindu God of preservation. Consort to the Goddess Lakshmi.

Vishuddhi Chakra: Chakra at the throat relating to the power of expression.

Vispassana: A Buddhist meditation technique that focuses primarily the awareness of breath and sensation to move beyond the mind.

Vortexes: Centers of power and/or swirling energy.

Wand: Spiritual tool for directing energy

Weak Nuclear Force: One of the four fundamental forces of nature. It is a short-range force, limited to distances smaller than an atomic nucleus.

Witness Based Awareness: A practice in which the practitioner is attempts to be perpetually aware of the play of the mind, by examining the quality of his or her thoughts.

Wraith Energy: This wraith energy exists through the focused intent of beings working together. The connection itself takes on an entity-like energy. This entity does not have a will of its own, but draws from the will and intelligence of the beings it connects.

Yang: Active, electrical, or masculine energy.

Yantras: A yogic based visual meditation image representing a Hindu deity or sacred syllable set used to focus and transform consciousness.

Yaqui: a Native American people who live in region comprising the northern Mexican state of Sonora and the southwestern U.S. State of Arizona.

Yin: Receptive, magnetic, or feminine energy.

Yoga: The path of union of the individual atma (soul) with Paramatma, (the universal soul) through the integration of body, mind, and spirit.

Yoga Sutras of Patanjali: One of the six philosophies of Vedic thought. It is a set of aphorisms (short phrases) that have been enormously influential regarding several branches of yogic theory and practice.

Index

Goddess 7, 30, 31, 32, 44, 160,
    194, 213- 214, 217, 218, 220
Golden mean 216
Golden Shadow 119, 214
Gratitude 92, 93
Greek
    43, 44, 80, 212, 213, 214, 215
Grounding Energy 93
Guilt   27, 116, 146, 149

H

Habits 21, 48, 73, 84, 96, 101,113
    144, 145
Happiness 40, 127, 169, 193, 194
Hara 11, 38, 119, 147, 214, 215,
    216, 217
Harmonic Proportions 189
Hatha Yoga 39, 214
Hatred 117, 118, 146
Haunted house 61
Healed feminine energy 29
Healed male energy 29
Healer 1, 62,136,153, 172, 200,203
Healing 4, 29, 30, 31, 32,33, 34,
    37, 44, 48, 50, 52, 55, 59,
    62, 63, 75, 83, 86, 91, 94,
    100, 102, 104-107, 131-133,
    135, 136, 144, 146, 147, 153,
    154, 167, 171, 173, 186, 200,
    202-204, 215, 218-220
Healing Meditation 104
Heart chakra 99, 104, 123, 150,156
Hecate 43, 214
Herbs 33, 69, 76, 88, 181, 218
    146, 147
High Self 44, 46, 47, 48, 50, 51,
Hindu /Hinduism 38, 43, 57, 80,
    147, 148, 160, 195, 212,214,
    215, 217, 218, 195, 220
Hinduism 80, 195
Holistic 3, 4
Holographic 16, 116, 214
Holographic Perception 214
    106, 125, 133, 135, 159, 212

Holy Ghost 43
Homosexuality 36
Humanitarian 165, 218
Humor 97, 113, 198
Huna 44, 207, 212, 215, 219, 220
Hyper-oxygenation 146
Hypnotherapy 2, 48, 215

I

Ida 38, 39, 40, 41, 152 215
Imagination 53 54, 90,115,135, 152
Imago Match 35, 213, 215
Immortal 144, 154, 173
Immortality 173
Incarnation 59, 60, 62
Incense 34, 69, 86, 87, 88, 90, 212
India 13, 121, 194, 198, 216-218
Indian 13, 85, 198, 216, 217
Indigenous 51, 135, 211, 218
Individuation 79, 199, 212, 213
Infancy 26
Initiates 31, 32, 33, 34, 86, 215
Initiation 52, 72, 73, 79, 86
Inner Child 104
Inner Judge 103, 108, 109,113,202
Innocence 70
Inspiration 5
Integrative spirituality 3
Integrity 197, 198, 215
Intellectual 19, 45, 65- 68, 72, 85,
    144, 170, 174
Intention 82, 90, 191, 13, 17,
    80-85, 87, 89, 90, 97, 102, 136
    137, 148, 161, 178, 182,
    191-193, 197, 217
Interconnectedness 192, 215
Intimacy 25, 26
Intuitive 45, 68, 75, 91, 170, 200,
    212
Involutionary 54, 56-58, 191, 215

J

Jackson Pollock 215

Order Form

Fax orders: (888) 393-6879. Send this form.

Telephone orders: Call 866-357-1843

Email orders orders@triplemuse.com

Postal Orders: Triple Muse Publications, PO Box 50667
Henderson, NV 89014 USA

Please send me the following books and CD's by Sylvia Brallier:

☐**Dancing in the Eye of Transformation**

$14.95 x _____ # of copies

☐**Companion Meditation CD for Dancing in the Eye of Transformation**

$14.95 x _____ # of copies (© September 2006)

Mp3 version sent via electronic transfer. $9.95 x _____ # of copies.

☐**Awakening the Sacred Fire World Trance CD**

$14.95 x _____ # of copies

Mp3 version sent via electronic transfer $9.95 x _____ # of copies.

☐**A Cosmology of All Being**

A booklet describing the beings of non-ordinary reality who assist us.

$6.00 x _____ # of copies

☐**Full size reproductions note cards of the illustrations in this book may be purchased through www.kivasingh.com**

Please send FREE information about:

☐Meditations CD for Dancing in the Eye of Transformation

☐Seminars and Retreats ☐Mailing list ☐Consultation

Name:_____

Address:_____

City: _____State_____ Zip: _____

Email_____

Sales tax: Please add 7.5% of total for products shipped to Nevada

Shipping by Air to the USA: $4.25 for the first book or disc and
$2.00 for each addt'l product. **International:** $10 for the first book
or disc, $5.00 for each addt'l product.

Payment: ☐Check   ☐Credit card:

☐Visa ☐Master Card ☐Optima ☐AMEX

Card Number:_____

Name on card: _____Exp.Date:_____